...Why

- Visit
- Invest
- Trade
- Shop
- Return
- Work
- Live
- Believe

1000

Numbers & Reasons

Why Dubai

DEDICATION

We dedicate this Book to

His Highness
Sheikh Mohammed Bin Rashid Al Maktoum
Vice President and Prime Minister of the UAE, and Ruler of Dubai

The visionary making Dubai what it is today
and what it will become tomorrow

Acknowledgement

We would like to thank Dubai Chamber of Commerce and Industry (DCCI) and each member of its management and staff who believed and supported us in this project from the beginning. Also, we would like to thank Beirut Information and Studies Center (BISC) and "Business Info"- Dubai teams and all the other contributors who devoted effort, time and hard work over the past 18 months to create this book.

1000 Numbers & Reasons Why Dubai
1st Edition - 2006

1000

Numbers & Reasons

Why Dubai

Publisher & Editor-in-Chief
Khaled Kassar

Managing Director
Mirna Ishac Chikhani

Head of Research Unit
Ghada Hassan

Chief Staff Editor
Dalia Chehab

Senior Editor
Lucia Dore

Researchers
Carine Joun
Mohamad Jamil
Iman Kebbi
Shadi Ghanem
Hania Taan
Chantal Raad

Research Supervisor
DCCI

Marketing Manager
Danielle Aychouh

Design & Layout
Lynn Zarif

Staff Assistants
Tarek Sheikh Najib
Yasser Ibrahim

Printing
Emirates Printing Press
Al Quoz, Dubai, UAE

In Association with:

BUSINESS INFO

P.O.Box 117546 Dubai, U.A.E
Al Murooj Rotana Offices, Off Sheikh Zayed Road
Tel: +971 4 3073723, Fax: +971 4 3215202
E-mail: info@businessinfo.ae

Published by:

BISC

P.O.Box 13-6600 Beirut, Lebanon
Hamra, Tour de Lyon, 4th floor
Tel: +961 1 355111, Fax: +961 1 355110
E-mail: bisc@bisc.com.lb

Co-publisher:

غرفة تجارة وصناعة
دبي

D U B A I
CHAMBER OF COMMERCE & INDUSTRY

CONTENTS

DCCI's Message

"1000 Numbers & Reasons Why Dubai" is a new idea designed not only for economists and investors but for all readers - whether students, entrepreneurs, or tourists - who wish to learn more about Dubai.

Unique and resourceful, this publication offers a new perspective from which to appreciate Dubai's development, its path to prosperity and the myriad of opportunities available to those who want to seize them, in an environment built on trust, cooperation and confidence.

Mainly, it covers events from the beginning of 2005 until the end of the first quarter of 2006 and the aim is to give readers an instant glimpse into this Emirate's growth and trends, along with its associated statistics, and numbers.

This publication is an overview of all Dubai's leading sectors. Most importantly, by simply opening any page, readers will be able to answer Why Dubai? Why Come to...Work...Invest...Visit...Stay...or Live...

DCCI continuously aims to improve interaction and knowledge-sharing services within the local and international business communities. Therefore, this publication ideally provides added value to local, regional and international investors, organizations, government institutions, entrepreneurs and individuals in the form of easy-to-use information that may assist in presentations, conferences and corporate annual reports.

Accordingly, DCCI will update **"1000 Numbers & Reasons Why Dubai"** each year. The publication will include coverage of Dubai's booming sectors in addition to other value-added and knowledge-based chapters. Each edition will evolve as we respond to our readers' feedback and recommendations.

With this publication, DCCI acknowledges that this Emirate has some of the world's greatest visionaries who continually find ways to advance the country's achievements and enhance its unique characteristics. Their contributions cannot be quantified.

Finally, by considering these data, we hope that readers will be encouraged to participate in Dubai's prosperous future.

Abdul Rahman G. Al Mutaiwee
Director General, DCCI

PUBLISHER'S MESSAGE

I believe in Dubai. The cosmopolitan haven for business, tourism, shopping, fine cuisine, nightlife, sports and the home to 180 nationalities, living together in a multilingual and multicultural city of prosperity and success.

Dubai is at the crossroads of three continents, where you can meet and chat with people from all over the world and all walks of life. Statesmen, sportspeople, key businessmen, internationally renowned personalities and many others flock to this extraordinary magnet of a place.

Dubai is where Paulo Coelho sells 4,000 books in an overnight visit. Dubai is where you move to and instantly feel at home. Dubai is where you can invest and your investments are realized. Dubai is where you can find the most ambitious and talented youth and gifted Arab women in the region.

It is the city of gold, golf, brands, sand dunes, palms, beaches and deserts; a place where you can dream and where dreams come true; a place where you can make the seemingly impossible happen.

Every fact or figure of each new project in Dubai is nearly always out-numbered or out-bettered by another new project. Dubai seems only to deal with hyperbolic superlatives. It is where the tallest building, the world's biggest shopping mall, the world's finest hotel are all being constructed simultaneously, and where the world's largest fleet of aircraft will soon be in operation to welcome a projected 120 million passengers by 2010.

It took me a long time to work out how I would be able to communicate the best and most representative numbers and reasons why Dubai. It is a place where you are continually overloaded with information, events, announcements, and world record-breaking facts and figures. But in early 2005, I cracked it...I became devoted to capturing all these numbers and reasons in one single book – a book that would reflect the very essence of Dubai: its vision, its excitement, its dynamism and, most importantly of all, its can-do attitude...

In Dubai alone, there are over $125 billion worth of projects either under implementation or in the planning-and-approval phase. This corner of the UAE has 20% of the world's construction cranes and recorded 16% economic growth in 2005, outstripping that of China. Its vision has allowed it to build a $15 billion aerospace enterprise, a $33 billion World Central project, Palm Trilogy, towers, villages, non-stop emerging cities and free zones. Every 4 seconds, a container lands at Dubai Ports. Every 3 minutes, 1 flight takes off or lands at Dubai International Airport, which has an average of 112 weekly flights to the UK and over 40 to Beirut. Dubailand, twice the size of Orlando's Disney World, is being constructed to welcome 15 million visitors a year. That is a lot of projects for a small city and it's just the beginning...

Our philosophy at BISC and "Business Info" is: "*information is everything*". Nevertheless, this book is only a modest first effort with hopefully many other yearly editions to come. That is Dubai - always changing, always improving, never standing still. Exactly as His Highness Sheikh Mohammed Bin Rashid Al Maktoum, Vice President and Prime Minister of the UAE, and Ruler of Dubai said in his outstanding book, "My Vision": "*In Dubai, there is no accurate development study available. This is not because we cannot prepare such studies, but rather because the pace of development is so fast that as soon as the study ends the current achievements would have been bypassed by much greater ones.*"

My intention is that by reading this book you will understand more about Dubai and you will be able to benefit from this wealth of information in your decision making, whether as a business person, a tourist, or simply a person eager for knowledge and endlessly hungry for more.

Dubai is exceptional; it is exciting; it is energetic; it has a vibrant pulse. I want everyone to know that.

Khaled Kassar
Publisher & Editor-in-Chief

REMARKS AND CLARIFICATIONS

1. An enjoyable read, **"1000 Numbers & Reasons Why Dubai"** aims to appeal and provide valuable information about Dubai and promote awareness for business people and investors, as well as to help discover business opportunities. The Book has 10 separate chapters, covering Dubai's key sectors as per the best suitable combinations of the latest available information.

2. The Book is not a statistical publication, but is intended to draw a colorful picture about Dubai, in a clear and creative visual presentation, backed by numbers, testimonials and quotations to interest a diverse readership.

3. The numbers and quotations gathered in this Book mainly cover the year 2005 and the first quarter of 2006.

4. The Book aims to mirror Dubai's growth throughout the mentioned period by providing the latest updates on an economy that expands daily.

5. The Book does not necessarily pretend to be a definitive reference of all statistics and quotations reflecting Dubai's growth.

6. Although the names and titles of corporate figures mentioned in the Book have been verified, in some cases the mentioned personalities may hold new or changed positions after the Book's publication.

7. Some data, numbers, quotations and projects may seem astounding or unbelievable to some readers, yet they actually quantify and state what has already happened, what is happening currently and what will be happening in Dubai. Furthermore, reliable sources have been used for each number and quotation mentioned in the Book and they can be seen in the Reference Pages.

DUBAI IN A NUTSHELL

Country: UAE
Dubai is the second largest among UAE's seven Emirates: Abu Dhabi (the capital), Dubai, Sharjah, Ajman, Umm al-Qaiwain, Ras al-Khaimah and Fujairah.

Area
Dubai has a total area of 4,114 square kilometers and the UAE's total area is 83,600 square kilometers (i.e. Dubai constitutes 4.9% of UAE area).

Location
Dubai lies on 55.16° longitude east, and 25.16° latitude north along the coast of the Arabian gulf extending 72 kilometers long, making it the UAE's most influential port and commercial center. The city of Dubai is divided by a water creek known as khor Dubai that is 13 kilometers long, and has a width between 100 meters and 500 meters.

Government
Regime: Federal
Leadership:
His Highness Sheikh Khalifa Bin Zayed Al Nahyan, President of the UAE and Ruler of Abu Dhabi
His Highness Sheikh Mohammed Bin Rashid Al Maktoum, Vice President and Prime Minister of the UAE and Ruler of Dubai.

Population
Dubai's population is estimated at 1.2 million people in 2005 and is forecast to reach 1.4 million people in 2010.

Nationalities
Dubai is a land of more than180 different nationalities.

Language
The official language of Dubai is Arabic. However, English is widely spoken and understood, with both languages being commonly used in business and commerce.

Average Temperatures (°C)
Minimum/Maximum
Jan: 14/24, Feb: 14/25, Mar: 17/28, Apr: 19/32, May: 23/37, Jun: 26/39, Jul: 29/41, Aug: 29/41, Sep: 26/39, Oct: 23/37, Nov: 18/30, Dec: 15/26.

Currency
AED or Dhs = UAE Dirham.
Notes: AED 1000, 500, 200, 100, 50, 20, 10 and 5.
Coins: AED 1, as well as 50 and 25.
Approximate Exchange rates:
US $1= AED 3.67
UK £1= AED 6.00

Local Time
Dubai is 4 hours ahead of GMT.

Economic Policy
The Government of Dubai is committed to liberal, free-market policies
and to the creation of a business environment conducive to commercial
activities.

Banking Hours
08:00-13:00. Closed on Fridays.
Exchange Houses: 16:30-20:30.

Shopping Hours
09:00-13:00 and 16:30-22:00.
Shopping Malls: 10:00-22:00.

Electricity
220/390 volts AC.

Heritage Sites
Sheikh Saeed Al Maktoum House, Dubai Museum, Hatta Heritage Village,
Heritage & Diving Village, Heritage House, Al Ahmadiya School and
Jumeirah Archaeological Site.

Dubai Landmarks
Dubai Chamber of Commerce and Industry, Burj Al-Arab, Clock Tower,
Corniche - (Hyatt), Creek & Yacht Club, Cruise Terminal, Madinat Jumeirah,
Dubai Internet City, Dubai Media City, Dubai International Financial Center,
Dubai Municipality, Dubai Duty Free, Dubai International Airport, Dubai
Courts, Emirates Towers, The Palms, Etisalat, Nad Al-Shiba Horse Racing
Court, Bany Yas Square (Naser Square), Port Rashid, Trade Center and
Union House.

MAJOR REASONS | 1

Major Reasons

The dynamic city that never sleeps. Where to go, who to meet, what to see, where to stay, what to invest in and most importantly what not to miss. With so many reasons yet so little time, this chapter provides you with the essential overview.

If you want to know why Dubai is such a thriving metropolis, why it has the most unbelievable man-made structures, and soon, the tallest building in the world – why in fact it attracts so many people from across the globe every day – the following pages are just a start.

"Most of people talk, we do things. They plan, we achieve. They hesitate, we move ahead. We are living proof that when human beings have the courage and commitment to transform a dream into reality, there is nothing that can stop them. Dubai is a living example of that."

HH Sheikh Mohammed Bin Rashid Al Maktoum, Vice President & Prime Minister of the UAE and Ruler of Dubai

OVERVIEW |

1 | A visionary leadership starting with the late HH Sheikh Rashid Bin Saeed Al Maktoum and flourishing under HH Sheikh Mohammed Bin Rashid Al Maktoum, Vice President and Prime Minister of the UAE and Ruler of Dubai.

2 | Dubai is one of the safest cities in the world.

3 | An oasis of political stability and prosperity since the country's establishment.

4 | A fair judicial system.

5 | Liberal economic system.

6 | Tolerant laws and regulatory conditions.

7 | Stable and diversified economy with promising indicators.

8 | No corporate tax, no income tax.

9 | No foreign exchange controls, trade barriers or quotas.

10 | 100% repatriation of capital and profit.

11 | Freedom from bureaucracy and the least corrupt city in the region.

Major Reasons

12 | Stable currency ($1 = AED 3.67).

13 | Freedom of living, freedom of speech and freedom to create.

14 | Most technologically developed city in the region.

15 | Pioneer in e-government and e-commerce.

16 | A magical façade of world investment and capital.

17 | A youthful economy with high levels of maturity.

18 | A government policy that facilitates Dubai staying ahead of the game.

19 | A regional first-class import, export and re-export center.

20 | Successful businesswomen and highly talented young females.

21 | The most attractive hub for the best and brightest minds in the Middle East and one of the best in the world.

22 | Knowledge-based society.

23 | Aviation hub of the region with one flight taking off or landing every 3 minutes.

24 | Dubai International Airport ranks 5th in the world.

25 | By 2010, Dubai will operate the largest airport in the world.

26 | A tourism powerhouse and leading transit destination.

27 | Dubai is expected and prepared to absorb hundreds of thousands of residents and some 15 million tourists and 120 million passengers by 2010.

28 | Strategically located at the crossroads of three continents (Europe, Asia and Africa).

29 | Dubai is the Middle Eastern center for world-class exhibitions and conventions.

Major Reasons

30 | Welcoming society and friendly locals.

31 | Secure environment for women and families 24/7.

32 | A place where traditional hospitality meets a modern and vibrant environment.

33 | An extraordinary leisure destination, with topnotch beach resorts and desert safaris.

34 | Open capital markets and diverse industries.

35 | Strong investor incentives and protection.

36 | 20 world-class free zones, with 100% foreign ownership, 100% commercial levies, 100% corporate tax exemptions and 100% import & export tax exemptions.

37 | Population growth of around 6% per annum.

38 | Set up a business in less than half the time of the regional average.

39 | Dubai is No. 1 business city in the GCC countries according to the latest Economist Intelligence Unit (EIU) survey.

40 | No other alternative business city in the region for at least the next 10 years.

41 | Dubai holds the 1st position in the Middle East for attracting international investment banks, companies, institutions, NGOs and other.

42 | Dubai was ranked 2nd in terms of transparency according to a report by the Economic & Social Commission for Western Asia (ESCWA).

43 | Leading Arab city in creativity and innovation.

44 | Ideal destination for entrepreneurs and fresh graduates.

45 | Around 79,470 companies are registered at Dubai Chamber of Commerce and Industry (DCCI) by the end of 2005.

46 | Competitive import duties (5% with many exemptions).

Major Reasons

47 | Dubai imports more than two thirds of the UAE's needs.

48 | Quick decision-making is the key to Dubai's success.

49 | Respect for human rights.

50 | A financial hub that combines the strength and role of Hong Kong and Shanghai.

51 | The ideal regional hub for Islamic banking and the financial industry generally.

52 | Highly developed and sophisticated infrastructure for all economic sectors.

53 | Dubai has been awarded "The Best Transport Infrastructure" in the Middle East.

54 | Abundant and inexpensive energy.

55 | Dubai is the ideal place to meet key decision-makers from all over the world.

56 | Trustworthy city that delivers what it promises.

57 | Highest international standards in business, construction, tourism and lifestyle.

58 | Commitment to values, ethics and corporate citizenship.

59 | Promoter of high corporate governance standards.

60 | Recognized as the 5th quality hub of the world and the headquarters of the Middle East Quality Association.

61 | Initiator and enforcer of the 1st regional customs unit to fight intellectual property rights violations.

62 | Dubai was ranked 18th among the top 20 cities in terms of digital governance, making it 1st among its Arab peers.

63 | Dubai recorded a 98% mobile phone penetration rate, higher than the world average, and awarded "Best IT and Telecommunications" in the Middle East.

Major Reasons

64 | One of the lowest crime rates in the world.

65 | The most competent and well-organized police force in the Arab world.

66 | Dubai Police is the 1st Arab Police Force to apply DNA testing in criminal investigations, use electronic printing and implement the paperless department concept.

67 | Clean city, green and well-governed environment and number 1 winner of the Award for Greening in the Arab World.

INTERNATIONAL CITY |

68 | Land of more than 180 nationalities and cultures.

69 | Progressive, tolerant, multilingual and multicultural city.

70 | A dynamic market for thousands of international brands.

71 | Regional home to more than 25% of Fortune 500 companies.

72 | International business recognition.

73 | Member of the World Trade Organization (WTO).

74 | Dubai has very strong foreign economic ties and business partnerships in addition to extensive trade relations with more than 165 states.

75 | Named the Middle Eastern **City of the Future** by "FDI" Magazine.

76 | **City of Gold:** The Dubai Gold and Commodities Exchange (DGCX) is the 1st commodities exchange in the Middle East.

77 | Dubai gold imports were worth $10.5 billion in 2005 and are expected to double in 5 years and retail trade reached $3 billion. Dubai will host the world's largest gold Souq.

78 | **City of Sports:** Dubai Sports City is a 50 million sq. ft project with the capacity for hundreds of thousands of spectators, to be completed in 2008.

Major Reasons

79 | Dubai's Sports events include Dubai Desert Classic, Dubai World Cup (the world's largest prize for a single horse race), Dubai Desert Challenge, UIM Class 1 World Powerboat Championship, Dubai Marathon, Dubai Tennis Championship and Dubai Rugby 7's.

80 | **City of Hotels:** Dubai is at the top of the world league for hotel occupancy averaging 85% and reaching 98% at peak times.

81 | 300 current hotels and around 150 new hotels are planning to open in Dubai by 2010, out of which 35 to 40 hotels will appear by 2008.

82 | Burj Al Arab, the world's only 7-star hotel, is as high as the Eiffel Tower at 321 meters and has the world's tallest atrium, at 180 meters.

83 | **City of Exhibitions:** The meetings, incentives, conventions and exhibitions (MICE) sector is one of the largest contributors to Dubai's growing tourism industry, and is one of the main contributors to Dubai's GDP.

84 | Dubai International Convention and Exhibition Center (DICEC) is the premier venue for exhibitions and conferences in the wider Middle East region, and more than 200 meetings, exhibitions, conferences, forums and workshops are organized in Dubai each year, where around half of them take place at DICEC.

85 | In terms of industry events, Dubai covers every important sector, and it is raising the bar with highly successful events such as: Dubai Air Show, Gitex, Index, ATM, etc.

86 | **City of Conferences:** Dubai hosted in the last years the best conferences in the world such as the World Bank Group and IMF Annual Meetings in 2003, the 40th International Advertising Agency (IAA) in 2006, Leaders in Dubai and Young Arab Leaders.

87 | **City of Festivals:** Dubai Shopping Festival (DSF) is the premier family activity event in the Middle East and hosts 3.3 million visitors who spend almost $2 billion yearly.

88 | **City of Entertainment:** Dubai Summer Surprises (DSS) is the most successful summer family event in the region.

89 | **City of Shopping:** An incredible place for shopping that attracts millions of visitors annually to its ultra-modern shopping malls.

Major Reasons

90 | 75% of the new shopping malls planned in the Gulf region will be located in Dubai.

91 | Mall of Arabia (part of City of Arabia), due to open in 2008, will be 10 million sq. ft when completed, making it one of the world's biggest malls.

92 | The largest mall in the world in 2009, Dubai Mall, will be 12.1 sq. ft with 16,000 car spaces and is expected to attract over 35 million visitors in the first year of operation.

93 | **City of Finance:** With a regulatory environment modeled on London and New York, the Dubai International Financial Center (DIFC) provides investors with all the assurances they would expect in a credible capital market.

94 | The Dubai International Financial Exchange (DIFX), with its European character, is a bridge between its members' regional countries and the rest of the world.

95 | **City of Media:** Dubai Media City (DMC) houses more than 1,000 companies comprising publishing houses, TV stations, broadcasting corporations, media and advertising.

96 | Dubai has all the logistics, services and resources of the world's major international business centers to establish a new venture.

AMAZING ECONOMY |

97 | An annual Gross Domestic Product (GDP) growth of between 13% and 21%.

98 | A total GDP of $37 billion in 2005, increasing from $30.15 billion in 2004 and $26.63 billion in 2003.

99 | An expected GDP of more than $41 billion in 2006.

100 | An average income per capita of $29,000, up from $24,000 in 2004.

101 | The fastest growing city in the region and among the highest growth rates in the world over the last decade.

102 | Dubai generates 73% of the UAE's non-oil revenues.

Major Reasons

103 | The least reliant on oil revenues among the GCC countries with non-oil GDP amounting to approximately 94%.

104 | Dubai's non-oil GDP has grown at an annual average rate of 5.8% in real terms between 1985 and 1993, 9.2% from 1993 to 2003, and reached more than 13% from 2003 to 2004.

105 | Recent DCCI estimates show that Dubai's non-oil GDP growth rate is sustainable and will continue at an average rate of 9.6% a year up to 2010.

106 | In 2006, Dubai government's budget showed a surplus of $1.5 billion.

107 | Around 40% of Dubai's 2006 budget is allocated for infrastructure.

108 | A property market that is likely to expand between 20% to 30% in 2006.

109 | By 2012, Emirates Airline expects to carry 33 million passengers annually on around 150 aircraft.

110 | Dubai is among the few cities in the world to apply the open-skies policy, allowing more than 112 airline companies to operate to and from Dubai.

111 | Emirates Airline is the best carrier in the Middle East and Africa Award winner for the 3rd consecutive year and winner of more than 270 world awards.

112 | In less than 1 hour, visitors get an entry visa into Dubai.

113 | Dubai Duty Free was awarded "The Best Airport for Duty Free Shopping Worldwide".

114 | Dubai Airport occupies 18th place in the world in terms of volume freight mobility and 2nd in terms of growth rate.

115 | By completion in 2007, Dubai International Airport will be positioned among the top 6 world airports in terms of cargo capacity.

116 | Dubai is establishing a $15 billion Dubai Aerospace Enterprise (DAE), a global aerospace manufacturing and services corporation.

Major Reasons

117 | Trade portal for volume exceeding $150 billion on a yearly basis and serving around 2 billion consumers.

118 | Dubai's growing global trade is estimated to cross $68 billion in 2010.

119 | More than 7.6 million containers are discharged annually in Dubai.

120 | A 9.5 million TEUs (20-foot Equivalent Units/Container) handling capacity in the existing Jebel Ali Terminal 1 is expected to increase to 15 million TEUs a year by 2008.

121 | A handling capacity of 55 million TEUs a year is expected by the year 2030 for Dubai Ports Authority (DPA).

122 | Dubai Ports World (DP World) is ranked the 7th largest container terminal operator worldwide, while its flagship facility of Port Rashid and Jebel Ali in Dubai are together ranked 9th.

MAGIC OF CRANES |

123 | Dubai is the most spectacular building experiment the planet has ever seen.

124 | More than 20% of the world's construction cranes work around the clock in Dubai.

125 | As if competing in an unofficial architectural Olympics, Dubai is striving to break as many records as it can in terms of "tallest", "largest", or simply, "first".

126 | Real estate experts estimate the value of investments and plans in Dubai's real estate at not less than $125 billion by early 2006.

127 | Dubai has made a commitment to health in the form of Dubai Healthcare City (DHCC). It is committed to attracting the best talent from around the world, providing the best medical care, medical research and education center in the region.

128 | Dubai's latest tourist landmark, Culture Village, is a $13.6 billion project which will be built along the Dubai Creek over an area of 40 million sq. ft.

129 | Dubai Festival City combines a world-class and unmatched mix of entertainment,

Major Reasons

dining and shopping. Upon its completion in 2011, the project would have a total initial cost and investment of around $10 billion.

130 | Dubailand will be the region's biggest tourism resort and one of the top 5 destinations in the world for family entertainment and leisure, with announced investments for 24 mega projects reaching more than $12 billion.

131 | Dubai will be home to the largest private sector project in the Middle East, "City of Arabia" (part of Dubailand), which includes Mall of Arabia, Wadi Walk, Elite Towers and Restless Planet and a dinosaur theme park.

132 | Dubai will host Aqua Dunya, a $1.9 billion gigantic water theme park resort, the largest in the Middle East.

133 | Dubai Snowdome, the $1 billion project that is the world's 3rd largest indoor ski resort and the only one in the Middle East.

134 | The Palm Islands are the 1st man-made projects since the Great Wall of China to be visible from space.

135 | "The World", to be completed in 2008, comprises exclusive paradise islands, that can only be reached by boat.

136 | On-going projects, including "The Palm Islands" and "The World", will triple Dubai's coastline to 81 million sq. m of mixed-use landmark development.

137 | Dubai Maritime City, to be completed in 2006, is the world's largest maritime development.

138 | Due for completion by the end of 2008, Burj Dubai will be the world's tallest tower and the centerpiece of the 500-acre, $8 billion "Downtown Dubai" development.

139 | Burj Dubai's area promoted as "Downtown Dubai" will be the most prestigious sq. km on the planet.

140 | The Dubai Metro, a $4 billion project, is projected to carry approximately 1.2 million passengers on average per day and 355 million passengers per year.

Major Reasons

141 | Dubai World Central is a pioneering new air transport hub that will transform the region into one of the most powerful global centers for logistics, tourism and commerce, and will be the world's 1st multi-modal logistics transport platform.

142 | Once completed, the new Jebel Ali Airport, an $8.1 billion project located in Dubai World Central, will serve 120 million passengers and 12 million tonnes of cargo annually.

143 | Dubai Logistics City is the world's largest multi-modal logistics hub for air, sea and road services. When Dubai Logistics City is completed, it will add 7 million tonnes of cargo capacity per year, one of the biggest cargo handling capacities in the world.

DUBAI IS LOCATED IN A COUNTRY ...

144 | Dubai is located in a country that achieved a GDP growth in nominal terms of 26% in 2005 according to the Ministry of Economy and Planning.

145 | Dubai is located in a country that has the fastest growing economy in the world with a nominal GDP growth in 2005 reaching AED 485 billion ($132 billion).

146 | Dubai is located in a country that proved all round growth particularly in the non-oil sectors, which showed a surge of 18.6% to $85 billion in 2005 from $71.6 billion in 2004, contributing by 64.3% to the GDP.

147 | Dubai is located in a country whose GDP is expected to reach $152 billion in 2006, according to the International Monetary Fund (IMF).

148 | Dubai is located in a country that has achieved a budgetary surplus of AED 38.2 billion ($10.4 billion) in 2005 against a deficit of AED 1.5 billion ($408 million) in 2004, according to the 2005 Economic Performance Report published by the UAE Ministry of Economy and Planning.

149 | Dubai is located in a country whose balance of payments achieved an overall surplus of AED 12.8 billion ($3.5 billion) in 2004 compared to a surplus of AED 4.7 billion ($1.3 billion) in 2003.

Major Reasons

150 | Dubai is located in a country where domestic and foreign investments in new projects are predicted to remain strong, while capital spending on real estate and infrastructure schemes will also stay high, according to the Economist Intelligence Unit .

151 | Dubai is located in a country where foreign direct investments (FDI) reached around $18 billion in 2005, and are expected to remain at similar levels in 2006.

152 | Dubai is located in a country that was ranked 2nd in the Arab world for attracting foreign direct investments (FDIs) and 17th on the international level among 140 countries, according to an ESCWA report.

153 | Dubai is located in a country that is classified as the 41st worldwide in terms of absolute size of its tourism sector, 65th in terms of relative contribution to the national economy among a list of 174 countries, according to the World Travel and Tourism Council (WTTC).

154 | Dubai is located in a country that Moody's has given an A1 country credit rating for "countries ability to settle their debts."

155 | Dubai is located in a country where infrastructure projects are very safe because of the government shareholding.

156 | Dubai is located in a country that has natural gas reserves of 213.5 trillion cubic feet, the 4th largest in the world after Russia, Iran and Qatar, while Abu Dhabi holds the largest reserves of 198.5 trillion cubic feet (approximately 93% of the UAE total), according to the UAE Yearbook 2006 published by the UAE Ministry of Information.

157 | Dubai is located in a country that will become one of the world's largest exporters of Liquified Petroleum Gas by 2009.

158 | Dubai is located in a country that contains proven crude oil reserves of 97.8 billion barrels, around 10% of the world total according to the Energy Information Administration (EIA) 2005 statistics.

159 | Dubai is located in a country that has an expected oil products' income of $39 billion in 2005, according to the Emirates Banks Association annual report 2005. Central Bank figures indicate that the UAE earned AED 108.79 billion ($29.6 billion) from oil sales in 2004.

Major Reasons

160 | Dubai is located in a country that needs more than $10 billion investment to meet the growing energy consumption demand.

161 | Dubai is located in a country that is among the most competitive worldwide, ranking 16th according to the Global Competitiveness Report 2004-2005, outweighing advanced European and industrial countries.

162 | Dubai is located in a country that was ranked as the least corrupt in the Arab World, according to a report by Economic & Social Commission for Western Asia (ESCWA).

163 | Dubai is located in a country that is one of the highest per capita world record breakers, according to The Guinness World Records 2006.

164 | Dubai is located in a country that is ranked 2nd in the Arab level and 41st in the 2005 UN Human Development Index (HDI), rising from 49th place in 2004.

165 | Dubai is located in a country that was ranked 3rd in the Arab world in terms of economic freedom, according to the Canadian Fraser Institute.

166 | Dubai is located in a country that is ranked at the top of Middle Eastern countries with a score of 86% by the World Bank's financial governance effectiveness report.

167 | Dubai is located in a country that was ranked as the world's 7th largest for the financing of mega projects, and 2nd largest among the Arab World in 2005.

168 | Dubai is located in a country that was ranked 2nd as a rising star, 4th as the most improved, 5th as a business destination and 6th as a center for conventions, according to the Country Brand Index 2005.

169 | Dubai is located in a country that was among the top 10 countries in the world in terms of an increase in the consumer confidence indicator by ACNielsen, outweighing Singapore, the US and the UK. The UAE was ranked 9th after scoring 110 points (i.e. 12 points above the world average).

170 | Dubai is located in a country that has established a program of economic reform and liberalization that has received high approval ratings from key international bodies such as the International Monetary Fund (IMF) and the World Trade Organization.

Major Reasons

171 | Dubai is located in a country where the inflation level could fall to 5% in 2006, from nearly 6% in 2005.

172 | Dubai is located in a country whose IT services sector is expected to grow consistently between 11% and 12%, according to Dubai Internet City (DIC).

173 | Dubai is located in a country that was ranked 28th on a world scale and the top performer in the Gulf region in the Networked Readiness Index 2005, released by the World Economic Forum.

174 | Dubai is located in a country that has registered an impressive growth in the manufacturing sector, showing a 15% increase in 2004, reaching AED 45 billion ($12.26 billion).

175 | Dubai is located in a country where the manufacturing industry will play an increasingly important role in the national economy in the future, due to the existing availability of basic essentials such as infrastructure and communications, as well as the availability of resources to fund the acquisition of the appropriate technology.

176 | Dubai is located in a country whose tourism sector is expected to contribute 20% to its GDP by 2010.

177 | Dubai is located in a country that has a high youth density in the 25 to 40 age group.

178 | Dubai is located in a country that has signed and strictly implemented all international agreements against money laundering and terrorism finance.

179 | Dubai is located in a country where the measures adopted to regulate capital markets are compatible with those of international requirements and are aimed at combating money laundering.

180 | Dubai is located in a country that is a member of the World Intellectual Property Organization (WIPO) and whose government strictly enforces piracy and patent laws as well as the protection of creativity.

181 | Dubai is located in a country that seeks to establish very strong trading links with powerful allies such as EU, Russia and Australia.

Major Reasons

182 | Dubai is located in a country that is investing around $20 billion in airport development projects from more than $40 billion planned for the Middle East, Africa and the Indian Subcontinent.

183 | Dubai is located in a country that is opening up its markets and that believes in the proven idea that succeeding in global markets requires more competition and open domestic markets.

184 | Dubai is located in a country that aims to enhance transparency by guaranteeing free access to information.

185 | Dubai is located in a country where culture and heritage are highly important aspects of the Government's development priorities.

186 | Dubai is located in a country whose foreign policy is based upon a set of guiding principles laid down by the country's leadership, believing in the need for justice in international dealings between states.

187 | Dubai is located in a country that seeks to reinforce the rule of international law, and to support the implementation of internationally agreed conventions.

188 | Dubai is located in a country that is an active participant in a number of international organizations including WTO, World Bank, IMF, UN, OPEC and many other international and regional bodies.

189 | Dubai is located in a country that is interested in new agricultural techniques that can boost yields without adversely affecting the environment and human health.

190 | Dubai is located in a country where environmental responsibility underpins almost all relevant decision-making processes on a day-to-day basis.

191 | Dubai is located in a country that has ratified international agreements relating to women, including the Convention on the Elimination of All Forms of Discrimination Against Women, futher to enforcing Labor Law and Anti-Child Labor Regulations.

Major Reasons

REAL ESTATE | 2

Real Estate

BOOM... What more is there to say about the city that announces a new project each day? Around 20% of the world's construction cranes are operating in Dubai. Dubai will soon be home to the world's tallest building, Burj Dubai, soaring more than 2,000 feet into the sky, as well as the world's tallest commercial tower and tallest hotel apartments. To absorb the large number of new residents coming into the Emirate, Dubai will need more than 500,000 additional residential units in future years. A challenging task but one that Dubai is uniquely placed to achieve.

"As a developer, it's an incredible place. The stuff they're doing is amazing, they're limited purely by their imagination and the laws of physics. It's an area that's growing rapidly and it's where we want to be."
Donald Trump Jr., Vice President for Development and Acquisition, *The Trump Organization*

OVERVIEW |

192 | "There is no stronger belief in the saying, 'If you build it, they will come' than in Dubai."
International Herald Tribune

193 | Dubai issued in March 2006, Law No. 7 legalizing freehold ownership of land and property for the UAE and GCC citizens, while allowing the same rights to non-GCC expatriates to pre-designated areas that will be approved by the Ruler of Dubai. This law will enhance the contractors' confidence in real estate and non-GCC expatriates will be given the right to acquire freehold and 99-year lease property, in areas designated by the Ruler.

194 | More than 20% of the world's construction cranes are being used to build more than 100 new mega projects in Dubai.

195 | "The recent study published by the Dubai Chamber of Commerce & Industry, shows that Dubai's construction and building sector contributed 12.2% to the Emirate's non-oil GDP in 2004 and has risen to 27% annually."
Majed Hamad Al Shamsi, Vice-Chairman, *Dubai Chamber of Commerce and Industry*

196 | Real estate experts claimed that Dubai will need at least around 500,000 additional residential units in the next 10 years.

197 | "It is estimated that more than 195,000 residential units will be completed within the next 5 years in Dubai alone."
Stefan Hickmott, Vice President, *Abraaj Capital*

Real Estate

198 | Real estate experts estimate that around 100 office towers will be added to the real estate market by the end of 2006 and early 2007.

199 | With yields ranging from 7 to 12% (higher than most international markets), real estate continued to remain attractive as an investment class.

200 | The number of active construction companies in Dubai increased to 5,938 in 2005, according to Dubai Chamber of Commerce & Industry (DCCI).

201 | Among active construction companies in Dubai, contracting of civil engineering works represented 45% of all construction companies working in the sector followed by building completion with 33%, building installation 20% and site preparation 2%.

202 | Dubai property market continues to absorb the supply of property as it emerges. Real estate is now a large part of the dynamic UAE economy, and will help to sustain the booming economy in any oil price downturn. Moreover, much of this investment is from equity sources and not borrowed money, so it is unlikely to dry up and leave property uncompleted.

203 | "We always believe in the market forces. I am confident that prices will stabilize as buildings are completed."
Sultan Ahmed Bin Sulayem, Executive Chairman, *Nakheel*

204 | "From being a vehicle to get rich quick, the Dubai property market has matured into a classic long-term savings plan for local residents and nationals. And banks report strong growth in their mortgage business creating a true end-user market. But the days of the speculator are over, at least until the next boom."
AME Info

205 | "Though Dubai's property market is soft, it is a healthy sign for all of us. The market is largely free from speculators and now genuine buyers would be buying and selling property in the market and that's good for everyone. With the correction, only genuine developers with quality products and services will remain in the market. In about two years time, developers will be judged by the quality of the buildings and timely delivery. That works out well for us."
Wazir Ali Daredia, Chief Executive Officer, *Trident International Holding*

Real Estate

206 | "The over-zealous buy-at-all-costs approach to real estate of the last two years will make way for a more contained marketplace. This should not be seen as negative: it ultimately bodes well for Dubai as a sustainable real estate option."
W. Jonathan Wride, Managing Director, *Capital Partners*

207 | "Dubai's property market was dominated by regional investors, but it has the potential of attracting money from places like Korea and Japan by creating an environment that would appeal to East Asian investors."
Kwon Hong Sa, Chairman, *Bando Corporation*

208 | "There is an unprecedented growth in the real estate finance sector in the UAE and the region due to the increase in demand for property in most of the Emirates, Dubai in particular. I expect that the size of the real estate finance market locally will reach AED 10 billion ($2.72 billion) during 2006. I anticipate that the value of the property that has been or will be delivered during 2005 and 2006, would reach around AED 33 billion, compared to AED 3 billion in 2003."
Mohammed Al Hashimi, Managing Director and Executive Manager, *Amlak Finance*

209 | "Our research showed us that a good majority of investors here invest in real estate as a second home or holiday home option. We intend to tap this market and present a lucrative proposition through a property management option which will guarantee returns of up to a minimum 75% for investors thereby yielding high revenues even when apartments are not in use."
Abuali Shroff, Managing Director, *Sheffield Real Estate*

210 | "Dubai is experiencing a construction boom, with new buildings going up at a pace that rivals China's - and all this in an Emirate that is roughly the size of Yosemite National Park."
BusinessWeek

211 | "Dubai has been growing phenomenally and what is heartening to note is that amidst all the development, environmentally too things are changing for the better. For instance we witness regulations on compulsory thermal insulation in all buildings, and the movement to form a green building council to name but a few."
Habiba Al Marashi, Chairperson, *Emirates Environmental Group (EEG)*

Real Estate

212 | Dubai and the UAE markets for air-conditioning systems have grown to around $410 million in 2005 and are now expected to exceed $800 million by 2008. This growth is attributed to the construction sector, including mega residential projects, shopping malls, hotels and other commercial projects.

NAKHEEL |

213 | Nakheel has the largest real estate portfolio currently under development in Dubai, including the Palm Island trilogy, The World, Dubai Waterfront, Jumeirah Lake Towers, Jumeirah Islands, Jumeirah Golf Estates and International City, among others.

214 | While Nakheel has not officially announced the total cost of its projects' portfolio due to the rapid and constant pace of its new projects in Dubai, real estate experts claim that Nakheel's total portfolio exceeds $100 billion. Market experts estimate that the cost and investment for Dubai Waterfront may reach $40 billion, The Palm Jumeirah $5 billion, The Palm Jebel Ali $7.5 billion and The Palm Deira $12.5 billion.

215 | The **Palm Jumeirah** will measure approximately 5 km in length and 5 km in width. The **Palm Jebel Ali** will be 7 km in length and 7.5 km in width and The **Palm Deira** is an astounding 14.3 km in length and 8.5 km in the width. The Crescent surrounding Palm Jumeirah will measure approximately 11 km in length while the Crescent surrounding The Palm Deira will measure approximately 21 km in length.

216 | A new city will rise from the sea when The Palm Deira is complete. The luxurious offshore development will be home to more than 500,000 residents, and there may never be a need to return to the mainland as the city will include a host of malls, clubs and sporting facilities. The giant project is located on an 80 sq. km area, much bigger than Manhattan and almost twice the size of the other two Palms at Jumeirah and Jebel Ali.

217 | The Palm Jumeirah, to be completed in 2007, will have a "Dive Experience" and will have 4 key themed areas: "Snorkler's Cove", "The Lost City", "Dives of the World" and a "Spear Fishing Area". It is worth noting that 25% of buyers of the Palm are British.

218 | **The World**, Nakheel's $1.8 billion project, will cover 63 sq. km. Hotels, resorts and luxury villas will be spread across 300 islands which will triple Dubai's natural coastline, creating 232 km of beachfront.

Real Estate

219 | The **Trump Tower,** a 48-storey mixed-use hotel and residential building which lies within The Palm Jumeirah, is the 1st development on The Palm Jumeirah as part of the exclusive regional partnership between Nakheel and The Trump Organization. It is projected to cost $600 million.

220 | "Nakheel has formed a new hotel and resort investment company, Nakheel Hotel and Resorts that will invest AED 2.2 billion ($600 million) to develop 8 hotels in its first year of operations. Nakheel Hotel and Resorts will roll out 20 new hotels in 5 years."
James Wilson, Chief Executive Officer, *Nakheel Hotels & Resorts*

221 | Property developer Nakheel was voted the World's Leading Tourism Property Development Company at the World Travel Awards 2005. The awards were voted for by travel industry professionals worldwide in addition to more than 175,000 people from 200 countries.

222 | **Jumeirah Village** is a freehold residential development that will contain over 6,000 villas and townhouses, set amidst luscious landscaping and unsurpassed leisure and lifestyle amenities. Jumeirah Village is a 100% freehold property.

223 | **Dubai Waterfront** project, located 35 km south west of Dubai, is the world's largest waterfront development. It is an 81 million sq. m beachfront mixed-use destination, encompassing over 250 best-of-breed master planned communities.

224 | There are 10 areas in the Dubai Waterfront, and the 1st phase starts from **Madinat Al Arab** and will include the Tower 'Al-Burj' which will be one of the world's tallest buildings. Land sales of Madinat Al Arab were recorded at AED 15 billion ($4 billion), up until February 2006.

225 | It is expected that **Al-Burj** (750 m minimal height, completed by 2009) will rival Burj Dubai for the world's tallest building title. Consequently, the two tallest buildings in the world will be in Dubai.

226 | Dubai Waterfront forms the first phase of a larger effort, the **Arabian Canal,** a 75 km development. It will serve as the primary entrance to the Arabian Canal, which ultimately will provide long-term waterfront investment opportunities.

227 | For Dubai Waterfront, 600 km of roads (further than the distance of Dubai to Bahrain- i.e. 481 km) and 5 sq. km of coral reef (equivalent to 1,000 football pitches) will be created.

Real Estate

228 | "What we're building here is the Middle East's city of the future. My district of Madinat Al Arab is going to be the downtown area and the city's heart, much like Times Square in New York or Piccadilly Circus in London."
Khaled Issa Al Huraimel, General Manager of the Madinat Al Arab district

EMAAR |

229 | Emaar Properties is the World's No.1 real estate developer in terms of market capitalization of over $40 billion.

230 | Emaar's net profits for 2005 climbed 180%, to a record $1.2 billion from $460 million for the year 2004. The company also reported an impressive 59% rise in revenues to $2.2 billion, as compared to $1.4 billion for 2004.

231 | "Today, we have a new vision for Emaar. We call it 'Vision 2010'. In the year 2010, we envision Emaar to be not just the number 1 real-estate company, but one of the most valuable companies in the world beyond property development, irrespective of business activity with malls, leisure, healthcare and financial services acting as separate engines for growth. Emaar has committed to invest AED 17.93 billion ($4.8 billion) in cash in 2006 in the UAE and 9 other countries, with expected returns of 20-40% from these projects."
Mohammed Ali Alabbar, Chairman, *Emaar Properties*

232 | Emaar has several real estate projects in its primary market of Dubai in various stages of completion. These include Dubai Marina, Arabian Ranches, Emirates Hills, The Meadows, The Springs, The Greens, The Lakes, The Views and Burj Dubai.

233 | The **Old Town**, being developed by Emaar Properties, is a vibrant waterside community. It is a town within a city, promising a special way of life with the fusion of stalls, boutiques, parlours and coffee houses to enjoy by day and live music and outdoor restaurants at night.

234 | Emaar has a backlog of 23,000 residential and commercial units to be completed between 2006 and 2008 and a substantial landbank, granted by the government.

235 | Emaar has delivered more than 13,000 residential units in the freehold market in less than 3 years, marking nearly 11 deliveries per day - one of the world's highest.

Real Estate

236 | Burj Dubai
- World's tallest tower, to be completed in 2008
- $20 billion (AED 73 billion) development
- 22 million sq. ft of total development
- 30,000 homes
- 9 world-class hotels – a total of 2,000 keys, including the 160-room Armani Hotel
- 19 residential towers
- World's largest shopping mall, The Dubai Mall
- 3.7 million sq. ft of leaseable space within The Dubai Mall
- 16,000 covered car parking for The Dubai Mall
- 6 acres of parkland

237 | Burj Dubai will have the world's highest elevator installation. The Observatory Elevators (double deck cabs) will have the world's highest travel distance from the lowest to the highest stop and will be the world's fastest at 18 m/sec (40 mph).

238 | Emaar has teamed up with Giorgio Armani S.P.A to build and manage 10 **Armani hotels** and resorts across the world. The 1st Armani hotel will feature in Emaar's flagship Burj Dubai.

239 | Emaar has formed the Corporate Governance Advisory Council to establish sound and effective policies, rules and practices to govern the relationship of stakeholders, enhance its risk management and internal control systems.

240 | Emaar Properties, the UAE's largest publicly listed company, has strengthened its credentials as an Islamic compliant organization by appointing a Fatwa and Shariah Board (FSB) to ensure compliance, as part of its efforts to gain transparency across the company's projects and operations.

241 | Emaar is planning to aggressively expand into the retail sector with investments of over $4 billion to develop approximately 100 malls in the emerging markets of the Middle East, North Africa and the Indian subcontinent.

242 | "Commercial and residential rents in Dubai are set to retreat to realistic levels, and in the process stimulating further sustained economic growth."
Mohammed Ali Alabbar, Chairman, *Emaar Properties*

Real Estate

DUBAI HOLDING |

243 | "We have built a success story in a short span of time. In 10 to 15 years, we have put Dubai on the map."
HE Mohammed Al Gergawi, UAE Minister of *State for Cabinet Affairs* and Executive Chairman, *Dubai Holding*

244 | Dubai Properties company, a member of Dubai Holding, is developing the **Business Bay** Project at a value of $30 billion. The project also includes the establishment of offices, residential towers, hotels and gardens over a surface area of 64 million sq. ft. A new canal will be set up, and it will add 6 km to Dubai's khor (bay). The project will compete with similar business centers in the most important cities across the world.

245 | "Once completed, Business Bay, a city within a city and Dubai's new upscale commercial district, will create a new center or downtown in Dubai attracting more than AED 65 billion ($17.7 billion) in direct investments in 230 commercial and residential towers. Business Bay has been structured in such way that it would fulfill the needs of both multinationals and small businesses. There will be room for everyone, including small start-ups while others will focus on the high-end corporate."
Hashim Al Dabbal, Chief Executive Officer, *Dubai Properties*

246 | Rising more than 484 m, **Burj Al Alam** presents itself as the tallest commercial tower in the world by 2009. Of its 108 storeys, 74 will be dedicated to offices, and 27 will be taken up by hotels and serviced apartments. The rest will be filled by retail outlets.

247 | "Tipped to be the tallest and most incredible edifice dedicated to commercial space, Burj Al Alam in Dubai's Business Bay, is a freehold commercial tower which will be one of the world's tallest. With an AED 4 billion ($1.1 billion) investment, it will reflect Dubai's growing eminence in the world of business."
Ahmad Khoury, Chairman, *Fortune Group*

248 | There is growing demand for freehold commercial spaces and Dubai Properties have responded by coming to the market with a unique office tower building, **The Vision Tower.**

249 | Jumeirah Beach Residence project is made up of 40 residential towers, covering a total area of 5 million sq. ft. It will house 25,000 people and will have 6,700 apartments and 4 luxurious hotels with 1,400 rooms.

Real Estate

250 | **Sama Dubai**, an arm of Dubai Holding, is constructing AED 5 billion of infrastructure works for 'The Lagoons', its 70 million sq. ft Dubai Creek waterfront project and one of the biggest real estate developments being undertaken in Dubai.

251 | **The Lagoons** Project, a new waterfront project on the Dubai Creek, has several cultural attractions, including Dubai's 1st opera house, a planetarium, a museum, an art center and a theater.

252 | "For us, only the sky is the limit. We will see where the opportunities lie and then invest accordingly. We will have a presence in all the major global markets where we see opportunities."
Farhan Faraidooni, Chief Executive Officer, *Sama Dubai*

253 | **Tatweer,** a Dubai Holding company, is building the **Bawadi** project, an AED 100 billion ($27 billion) mega hospitality project that will be the largest hospitality and leisure development in the world with 35 themed hotels offering 29,200 rooms, 100 simultaneous plays and shows at different venues and more than 1,500 restaurants.

254 | The centerpiece of Bawadi will be the world's largest hotel, **Asia-Asia**, which alone will comprise 6,500 rooms, combining 5,100 4-star and an additional 1,400 5-star rooms. Asia-Asia will be a part of the first phase of development, which includes total spending of AED 12 billion by Tatweer in hotel and infrastructure, and will be completed by 2010.

255 | Tatweer will invest AED 40 billion ($10.9 billion) in the project, building the Asia-Asia and Bawadi's infrastructure, while the rest of the total investment needed will come from investors. Bawadi is expected to host 3.3 million guests by 2016 which in turn will represent more than 21% of the total number of tourists that Dubai expects to host by that time, according to Tatweer.

256 | "The launch of this project effectively signals the next major phase in tourism development in Dubai as we look forward to the next 8 years of major growth."
Saeed Al Muntafiq, Chief Executive Officer, *Tatweer*

257 | In terms of area, Dubailand one of Dubai Holding's main projects, will be twice the size of Orlando's Disney World, or the same size as the current built-up area of Dubai, with around 55 hotels and resorts offering up to 50,000 new rooms, creating the world's largest visitor destination, expecting 15 million visitors per year. (*More information about Dubailand and its projects are detailed in the Travel and Tourism Chapter*).

Real Estate

258 | Capital Partners, a US private equity firm that focuses on investment between the US and Dubai, has signed an agreement with Dubai Technology and Media Free Zone (Tecom), part of Dubai Holding, to develop a $1 billion building project in Dubai Internet City. **RiverWalk**, a car-free development in the heart of 'new' Dubai, will cover an area of more than 480,000 sq. m. It will comprise residential apartments, offices, boutiques, galleries, cafés and an international business hotel.

259 | "There is tremendous opportunity in the whole region. Multinational companies are also trying to share in the growth and are here to showcase their projects. Real estate is one of the biggest sectors in Dubai and the GCC."
HE Mohammed Al Gergawi, UAE Minister of *State for Cabinet Affairs* and Executive Chairman, *Dubai Holding*

OTHER PROJECTS |

260 | **Dubai Investments Park (DIP)**, a wholly owned subsidiary of Dubai Investments (DI), is a one of its kind residential and commercial zone with a total area of 8.7 million sq. m.

261 | "The number of companies in Dubai Investments Park (DIP), which is being developed by Dubai Investments in partnership with the Union Properties real estate company, has reached 366. This is expected to increase to 550 companies by the end of 2006 and investments in the development are forecast to increase to around AED 20 billion ($5.4 billion) by the end of 2008."
Khalid Bin Kalban, Managing Director and Chief Executive Officer, *Dubai Investments*

262 | **Some large-scale real estate projects are due to be built in Dubai International Financial Center (DIFC) in 2007 and 2008:**
  • One Central Park, AED 1.8 billion, 80 floors
  • Apartment Park Lane, AED 1.5 billion (residential)
  • Ritz Carlton, AED 1.5 billion, 18 floors, hotel (330 rooms)
  • Park Towers, AED 600 million, 2 towers (residential)
  • Guarantee Towers, AED 1.6 billion, 3 buildings (commercial, residential and hotel)
  • Two 26-floor towers, AED 450 million (residential and commercial)
  • Scan Gardens, AED 500 million, 47 floors (residential)
  • Al Fatan Tower, AED 450 million, 2 towers, 50 apartments (residential)
  • Liberty House, AED 450 million, 60 floors (commercial and residential)

Real Estate

263 | **Dubai Lagoon,** a residential community complex being built at the Dubai Investments Park, is located close to Dubailand and Sports City. The AED 3 billion ($817 million) freehold development project will be spread over 1.75 million sq. ft (162,000 sq. m) and contains 51 buildings consisting of studios in 8 different shapes and penthouse apartments.

264 | Dubai-based realtors **Al Manal** Development will invest AED 3 billion ($817 million) in a new residential community, Crown City, that will see 8,000 housing units comprising 52 buildings in the Dubai Investments Park (DIP).

265 | In 2005, **Union Properties** Company achieved net profits of AED 584.5 million ($159 million), an increase of 294% on the 2004 results of AED 148.41 million. The company's revenues increased by 144% to AED 1.388 billion ($351 million) from AED 569.9 million in 2004.

266 | In Dubai, **Tameer's** projects include the construction of the tallest residential tower in the world at Dubai Marina, called the **Princess Tower**. It is also building 2 residential towers at International City, known as Al Dana-1 and Al Dana-2.

267 | "We are one of the fastest growing companies in the region. We started this business in early 2003. To date (February 2006), our portfolio is around AED 40 billion ($10.8 billion). Our goal is to be the biggest real estate company in 5 years."
Omar Ayesh, Founder and President, *Tameer Holding*

INFRASTRUCTURE |

268 | **Dubai Municipality's** annual budget exceeds AED 1.28 billion ($350 million), with approximately 90% allocated to infrastructure development.

269 | Dubai plans to invest over AED 22 billion ($6 billion) in infrastructure-related projects in the medium term: AED 16.5 billion ($4.5 billion) is earmarked for the light rail and transit (LRT) development, around AED 1.83 billion ($500 million) will be spent on road and bridges, AED 1.1 billion ($300 million) on drainage and irrigation and AED 2.56 billion ($700 million) on general projects.

270 | Dubai's road network is under continuous expansion with over 20 major new projects under construction or recently completed, including a 1.5-kilometer tunnel under the

Real Estate

airport and a new 12-lane bridge across Dubai Creek. Work on the AED 388 million ($105.7 million) bridge project began in February 2005.

271 | "Based on available statistics for the current development projects, we are planning a road network for a projected population of 5 million people in Dubai excluding tourists."
Mattar Al Tayer, Chairman and Chief Executive Officer, *Roads and Transport Authority (RTA)*

272 | The **Dubai Metro** is an AED 15 billion ($4 billion) driverless, fully automated metro network project carried out by the Dubai Rapid Link (DURL), a consortium headed by Japan's Mitsubishi Corporation. The planned light rail network will consist of 2 lines with a total track length of 70 km.

273 | The Dubai Metro System, the largest ever infrastructure project in the GCC, will include 55 stations, 18 km of tunnels, 51 km of viaduct, one major train depot, a maintenance facilities site, several auxiliary stabling facilities and the total fleet size will be slightly in excess of 100 trains.

274 | Once in full operation, the Dubai Metro System is projected to carry approximately 1.2 million passengers on an average day and 355 million passengers per year. The system will handle 1.85 million travelers a day by 2020.

275 | "The Dubai Metro would cater to at least 17% of the projected 35% who will be using public transport, including buses and water transport. The number of cars registered in Dubai has already crossed the 600,000 mark and there has been an annual increase of 10%. This is in addition to vehicles coming to Dubai from neighboring Emirates and even other GCC countries. There are 3 cars for every 10 people. It means every 3rd person has a car in Dubai."
Mattar Al Tayer, Chairman and Executive Director, *Roads and Transport Authority (RTA)*

276 | At the end of 2005, a new law was issued, establishing The Roads & Transportation Authority that is charged with the responsibility of planning and undertaking road, traffic and transport projects in Dubai with a view to providing an efficient and safe integrated transportation system. This is in line with the other objectives of the decision-makers in Dubai to make the Emirate an attractive, secure and effective center of commerce.

Real Estate

277 | Dubai public transportation services include 411 buses deployed on 62 internal routes, covering an area of 3,885 sq. km. The buses cross 168,000 km (1,500 bus stops) and carry about 230,000 passengers every year.

278 | Statistics reveal that 36 million travelers have already used Dubai Municipality's transport systems.

279 | Even as the average daily trips in Dubai are anticipated to grow from 3.1 million per day to 13.1 million in 2020, Dubai's integrated transportation solution targets an increase of public transport market share from 4.7-17% over the next 15 years.

280 | Currently, there are 149 abras (water taxis) in operation through six stations in Dubai Creek. An abra is a traditional boat made from wood used to transfer people in the Dubai creek. It takes 10 minutes to go from Deira to the other side (Bur Dubai).

281 | "In 2004 around 16 million people used the abra but the number is expected to reach up to 22 million in 2005. The latest study showed that the abra users have increased from 7.9 million to 11.3 million during the first 6 months of 2005 compared to the same period last year."
Abdul Aziz Malek, Director of the Public Transport Department, *Dubai Municipality*

Real Estate

FINANCIAL MARKETS | 3

Financial Markets

In Dubai, money spins. 500 companies are expected to register at Dubai International Financial Center (DIFC) by 2010 and the Dubai Financial Market (DFM) is one of the world's few bourses that has operations open to the public. By the end of 2005, it had achieved annual growth of 219%, the highest growth among the Arab world's capital markets. Dubai is also a thriving commodities hub through Dubai Multi Commodities Center (DMCC), where Dubai Gold and Commodities Exchange (DGCX), has an increasing daily average turnover and is set to achieve an ambitious target of 20,000 silver futures contracts per day by the end of 2006.

"Today we will succeed in modifying the way the world perceives this region, and we will also change the way we look at the world. For the first time, international investment houses will find a center that they can trust in the Middle East."
Dr. Omar Bin Sulaiman, Director General, *Dubai International Financial Center (DIFC)*

OVERVIEW |

282 | The UAE securities market index grew by 110.3% reaching 6839.97 points in the year 2005. Shares market value rose by AED 519.5 billion ($141.5 billion) in 2005 to reach total of AED 839.68 billion including AED 105 billion (13%) representing additional share values entered to the market.

283 | The shares traded at the UAE securities market value reached AED 509.8 billion in 2005 reflecting a growth up to 661% comparing with AED 67 billion in 2004. The shares traded by sectors during 2005 are as follows: Services sector AED 385.5 billion, Banking sector AED 91.4 billion, Industrial sector AED 21.7 billion and Insurance sector AED 11.2 billion.

284 | Dubai Financial Market (DFM) is in the process of converting into a public shareholding company in which the government will contribute with 80% of its capital and the remaining 20% will be offered to the people an initial public offering.

285 | "The growing status of Dubai as a financial hub of the region gives the city the combined strength and role of Hong Kong and Shanghai put together, in the economic development of the Middle East and Africa. The huge infrastructure development taking place in Dubai will boost the region's economy as Shanghai did to the whole of China."
David M. Darst, Managing Director and Chief Investment Strategist, *Morgan Stanley*

286 | According to the Arab Monetary Fund, Dubai Financial Market topped the Arab capital markets in terms of annual growth that reached 219% by the end of 2005, in comparison with 2004. Abu Dhabi Securities Market (ADSM) came in 2nd place achieving a 138.6% growth in its market capitalization by end 2005.

Financial Markets

287 | Dubai Financial Market accounted for 82% of the value of shares traded on the UAE capital markets and Abu Dhabi Securities Market (ADSM) accounted for the remaining 18%.

DFM |

288 | "Dubai Financial Market is one of the world's few bourses which have operations open to the public. Since we opened the market before the public, we have to meet their aspirations and desires. The market suddenly had to absorb around 300,000 investors. Estimates revealed that 1% of them – or 3,000 – would come to the market, whereas in reality more than 7,000 investors have been present at the bourse every day in 2005." **Issa Kazem,** Director General, *Dubai Financial Market (DFM)*

289 | The total number of companies listed on Dubai Financial Market (DFM) was 35 and 52 securities in total by the end of March 2006.

290 | Annual statistics issued by DFM revealed an increase of 92% in the total number of investors in the market during 2005, to reach 297,610 investors in return for 155,076 investors in 2004. Investors came from 140 different countries, whereas in 2004, they came from 95 countries.

291 | The number of female investors increased by 70%, an increase of 30,000 women, according to DFM estimates for the first 11 months of 2005. The value of traded shares volume rose 990% to 1.457 billion shares with a value of AED 22,411 billion. This represents a 1700% increase on the same period in 2004. By the end of 2005, the number of female investors on the DFM reached more than 74,000 investors.

292 | Dubai and the UAE saw no less than 10 capital raising exercises (August-November 2005) through rights issues and IPOs. The total amount of liquidity thus raised is around $10 billion. This source of liquidity has fuelled DFM to record gains of 150%.

DIFC |

293 | An independent regulator, a judicial system based on a regulatory framework derived from international best practises, along with 2 billion consumers and $1.8 trillion of GDP in the region, Dubai International Financial Center (DIFC) offers a highly vibrant market to the international business community.

Financial Markets

294 | By the end of 2005, over 100 of the best known companies in the world had joined the DIFC, including Morgan Stanley, HSBC, Standard Chartered Bank, Argent Financial Group, Deutsche Bank, PricewaterhouseCoopers and KPMG, and the number is expected to increase considerably in 2006. Furthermore, the DIFC is expected to attract around 500 companies by 2010.

295 | "DIFC is creating a new center of gravity for the region's banking community which is attracting an increasing number of international financial institutions."
Stephen Green, Chief Executive, *HSBC Group* and Chairman, *HSBC Bank Middle East Limited*

296 | The DIFC has big ambitions, aiming to play host to 20% of the world's investment funds. It has enacted the collective investment law to provide a legal framework, covering mutual funds, property funds, Islamic funds, hedge funds and private equity funds.

297 | "The regulatory environment at the Dubai International Financial Center is modeled closely on London and New York and provides investors with the reassurances they would expect in a credible capital market. We have ambitious growth plans for this venture and are well placed with our customers here to develop a new branch in the DIFC."
Cormac Sheedy, Associate Director of the International Development Division, *Invesco*

298 | "The DIFC, as the newest international financial center, is an obvious choice of location for us to set up an office to complement our existing offices in Dubai, Sharjah and Abu Dhabi. As one of the 'Big Four' global accountancy firms, we are pleased to associate ourselves with this new development in Dubai and look forward to it, and therefore our success."
Vijendra Nath Malhotra, Senior Partner and Chief Executive Officer, *KPMG UAE*

299 | "Countries around the world are increasingly recognising the need to improve corporate governance standards. High standards for corporate governance enable countries to attract investment - domestic and foreign - and to provide jobs for their citizens. The establishment by the UAE government of **Hawkama** - the Institute for Corporate Governance, hosted by the Dubai International Financial Center (DIFC) - is a very timely initiative that will support national and regional efforts to improve corporate governance. The OECD is pleased to co-operate with this newly established institute in the context of the MENA-OECD Investment Program."
Richard E. Hecklinger, Deputy Secretary General, *OECD*

Financial Markets

300 | "This is a ground breaking and strategic initiative that will promote institution building for the countries of the region. It is vital that we bridge the corporate governance gap to achieve international economic and financial integration. Hawkama will belong to the region and ensure that sustainable corporate governance programs are developed and implemented."
HE Dr. Nasser H. Saidi, Chairman, *MENA-OECD Working Group on Corporate Governance*

301 | "In Dubai International Financial Center (DIFC), organizations providing financial services have the infrastructure, the information technology, the regulation, the legal framework and the resources to build a successful business."
Assem O. Kabesh, Chief Business Development Officer, *DIFC*

302 | DIFC reached the final stages of establishing a regulatory framework for Collective Investment Funds (CIF). The regulatory approach is recognizable to international regulators and adheres to the core principles laid down by The International Organization of Securities Commissions (IOSCO).

303 | "We have made a commitment to Dubai. When we looked at the region from the outside, it seemed the best place to be. Now we have realized that the gravity of financial services is shifting to Dubai so we have shifted our base to the DIFC."
Jon Little, Chief Executive Officer, *Global Mellon Investments*

304 | "Through the Dubai International Financial Exchange (DIFX), the DIFC will enable and facilitate the numerous privatizations planned in the region. It will provide a platform for the industry to seek international investment in a liquid, well-regulated environment. DIFC will also encourage merger and acquisition (M&A) activity to produce bigger and more competitive business units that are attractive to foreign ownership. Legal assurance will be provided by DIFC's court and judicial system where disputes can be tried under any established legal framework."
Dr. Omar Bin Sulaiman, Director General, *Dubai Financial Services Authority (DFSA)*

305 | Dubai International Financial Center (DIFC) has registered equity funds, offering companies an alternative to offshore hubs.

306 | Saudi Arabia's **Kingdom Holding**, owned by Prince Al-Waleed Bin Talal Bin Abdulaziz Al Saud, has registered a company – Kingdom Hotel Investments (KHI) – at Dubai International Financial Center (DIFC).

Financial Markets

307 | **Shuaa Capital** was licensed from the Dubai Financial Services Authority (DFSA) to provide a comprehensive range of banking investment services at DIFC. Thus, it becomes the 1ˢᵗ Arab and regional investment bank to get a license that empowers it to work as a financial broker and a member of clearance at Dubai International Financial Center.

308 | "It is a tremendous achievement for **Abraaj** to be the first pure private equity firm to be registered by the DFSA. This is doubly significant when you consider that we have never been a regulated business, and it is testament to the high standards of corporate governance that we adhere to that the DFSA has given us this license."
Arif Naqvi, CEO and Vice Chairman, *Abraaj Capital*

309 | The **National Investor**, is the 1ˢᵗ UAE based investment bank to receive a license to operate in the DIFC.

310 | **HSBC** announced it is relocating its regional investment banking headquarters to DIFC in early 2006.

311 | **National Bank of Kuwait** (NBK) Capital received the Dubai Financial Services Authority (DFSA) license to establish a presence in Dubai International Financial Center.

312 | The **Chartered Insurance Institute**, the largest institute for the training of insurance and banking services, was inaugurated in the Dubai International Financial Center. It is the 1ˢᵗ office of the Institute, to be ever established outside London.

313 | **Argent** Financial Group International, a UK subsidiary of the Argent Financial Group and an affiliate of the Argent Funds Group, has been licensed by the Dubai Financial Services Authority (DFSA) to operate as an authorized firm from the Dubai International Financial Center.

314 | **Carey Pensions & Benefits** received the Dubai Financial Services Authority approval to operate as a licensed Ancillary Service Provider in the DIFC.

315 | The International investment and advisory firm **Babcock & Brown** has been granted a license by the Dubai Financial Services Authority (DFSA) to operate as an authorized firm in the Dubai International Financial Center (DIFC).

316 | **Linklaters**, a law firm which specializes in advising the world's leading companies,

Financial Markets

financial institutions and governments on their most challenging transactions and assignments, has been registered by the Dubai Financial Services Authority (DFSA) to operate as an ancillary service provider from the DIFC. Linklaters now has 30 offices in 23 of the world's major business and financial centers.

317 | **Superfund** Investment Group opened their Middle East headquarters in the DIFC.

318 | "Dubai has recently become one of the world's most attractive financial centers. The Middle East is extremely important for the capital markets, particularly for managed futures funds. We are planning to implement numerous activities for the whole region out of Dubai."
Christian Baha, Founder, *Superfund Investment Group*

319 | Singapore's **DBS bank** recieved a license to operate at the DIFC and became the 1st Singaporean lending institution to access the Middle Eastern market.

320 | **Unit Trust of India** (UTI), the oldest fund manager in India, with $5.6 billion assets under management, has plans to set up operations in the DIFC through UTI International, its fully owned offshore subsidiary.

321 | "FTSE is honored to bring its international indexing expertise to this exciting new market. Our experience across Europe and Asia, including developing indices in accordance with Islamic investment principles, provides the basis from which we can create an index family to capture the specific requirements of DIFX's new market."
Donald Keith, Deputy Chief Executive, *FTSE Group*

322 | "Being a DIFC company allow Takaful Re to be in the heart of the most important and promising financial hub in the MENA region and to benefit from the existing infrastructure and facilities. The DIFC is one of the most efficient and well regulated environments in the Middle East. And, for Takaful Re, to be under the supervision of the DFSA is a label for transparency and corporate governance."
Chakib Abouzaid, Chief Executive Officer, *Takaful Re*

DIFX |

323 | "DIFX will enhance capital mobility in the region and attract new international capital. It will create additional regional and international opportunities at the doorstep of

Financial Markets

institutional investors here. At the same time, it will give issuers of securities access to capital in a financial environment that is comparable to Hong Kong or London."
Dr. Henry Azzam, Chairman, *Dubai International Financial Exchange (DIFX)*

324 | By March 2006, the Dubai International Financial Exchange (DIFX) had 12 members: Barclays Capital Securities, Credit Suisse Securities, Citigroup Global Markets, Deutsche Bank, HSBC, Morgan Stanley & Co. International, UBS AG, EFG-Hermes UAE, KAS Bank, Mashreq Capital DIFC Limited, Merrill Lynch and Shuaa Capital International.

325 | "Dubai International Financial Exchange (DIFX) is great news for us and our investors and announces a new era for the financial industry in the region. The possibilities will be tremendous as the market establishes a broad breadth of product range."
Mustafa Abdel Wadood, Chief Executive Officer, *EFG-Hermes UAE*

326 | "DIFX operations complete the cycle of the international financial system by covering regions which were not previously covered by the world financial centers, chiefly in Europe, the Far East and North America."
Abdul Aziz Al-Ghurair, Chief Executive Officer, *Mashreqbank*

327 | "DIFX is even more important because it offers some financial services that are not available in other countries in the region, including Shariah-compliant bonds and other instruments. It also enjoys transparency through clear market operations and an impartial governing authority. We expect 15 companies to list their shares through IPOs within 18 months from the day of the opening of the bourse. We also expect some 40 to 50 financial brokerage houses to operate by the end of 2006."
Nasser Al Shaali, Chief Operating Officer, DIFX

328 | "They are making every effort to become the New York Stock Exchange or London Stock Exchange of the region, and I believe they will succeed."
Jameel Akhrass, London-based Head of Middle East Investment Banking, *Morgan Stanley*

329 | "The fact that global insurance and financial services companies are listed on the DIFX will help boost confidence in the bourse and its capability to lure foreign capital and investments."
Dr. Omar Bin Sulaiman, Director General, *Dubai International Financial Center (DIFC)*

330 | "The measures adopted to regulate capital markets in the UAE cannot be breached and are meant to combat money laundering operations. The measures are compatible

Financial Markets

with international requirements, a matter which made the UAE ideal for investments. The UAE signed all international agreements against money laundering and terrorism finance, enforced by all UAE financial institutions, including DIFX."
Abdulrahim Mohammed Al Awadi, Head of Anti-Money Laundering and Suspicious Cases Unit, *Central Bank of the UAE*

331 | The Dubai International Financial Exchange (DIFX) has granted membership to **EFG-Hermes** UAE, the 1ˢᵗ regional institution to join the exchange as an Individual Clearing Member. EFG-Hermes, a leading investment bank in the region, was licensed by the Dubai International Financial Center (DIFC) in 2005.

332 | **Investcom** Holding has become the 1ˢᵗ company to list its shares on the Dubai International Financial Exchange (DIFX).

333 | "DIFX will bring international investment into regional securities on an unprecedented scale. By tapping into this investment, regional companies can obtain the capital they need to grow."
Steffen Schubert, Chief Executive Officer, *Dubai International Financial Exchange (DIFX)*

334 | **KAS Bank**, a European bank providing a wide range of securities and management information services, joined DIFX as a General Clearing Member further to offering sub-custodian services to users of the exchange. The core activities of the Bank are global custody, clearing and settlement for institutional investors and financial institutions.

335 | "Regional and international banks are attracted by the unique opportunities offered by DIFX. It will be the only exchange in the Middle East to have market makers, which will encourage liquidity. It is also the only one to have a central counter-party clearing system, which guarantees that trades are honored."
Nasser Al Shaali, Chief Operating Officer, *DIFX*

336 | "We believe that the Dubai International Financial Exchange (DIFX) is likely to spur the Initial Public Offering (IPO) market and will help increase the number of local companies approaching the capital market to raise funds. Family businesses are likely to go public on the DIFX by listing a minimum of 30% of their share capital. In addition, we believe that the abundant liquidity available in the region will attract a number of foreign companies approaching DIFX to float IPOs."
Global Investment House of Kuwait

Financial Markets

337 | "DIFX is unique in many terms as it has been developed to offer services to regional and international institutions at the same time. In the past, many global players had to leave the Middle East as they could not get a fair valuation. DIFX has filled that gap and now the institutions would get a fair chance to grow. The region is home to 2 billion people – nearly a 3rd of the world's population."
Fadi Ghosaini, Head of Business Development, *DIFX*

338 | Before the end of 2006, officials expect some 9 bonds, 5 sukuks and 10-15 IPOs to be listed on DIFX. The IPOs are expected to raise nearly $2 billion in funds from the GCC. Some 10 to 15 secondary listings from companies from India, Pakistan and South Africa are also expected.

339 | DIFX's rules may attract local companies to list because of its less stringent regulations. Companies floating an IPO on the DIFX will be required to offer only 25% of their shares to the public - much lower than existing local rules, which require 55% to be floated.

DFSA |

340 | In 2005, Dubai Financial Services Authority (DFSA) and Capital Markets Board of Turkey (CMB) signed a memorandum of understanding (MoU) for the cooperation and exchange of information between the 2 bodies in all sectors, chiefly in international financial crimes.

341 | DFSA agreed on a regulatory protocol with the Commodity Futures Trading Commission (CFTC) in December 2005.

342 | DFSA signed an agreement with the UK's Financial Services Authority formalizing cooperation and information sharing between the 2 regulators. It recognizes that both regulators place reliance on the quality of regulatory standards administered in the other's jurisdiction.

343 | DFSA has entered into a memorandum of understanding (MoU) with the **Jersey Financial Services Commission** (JFSC). The JFSC is responsible for the regulation and supervision of banking, collective investment funds, insurance business, investment business and trust company business in Jersey.

344 | DFSA has entered into a memorandum of understanding (MoU) with the Securities

Financial Markets

and Exchange Commission in Thailand (SEC). The agency is responsible for the authorization, registration and supervision of the issuance, offer or sale of securities and derivatives, market intermediaries related to securities and derivatives, exchange, and clearing & settlement entities.

DMCC |

345 | The Dubai Multi Commodities Center (DMCC) is a strategic initiative of the Dubai government created to establish a commodity marketplace in Dubai. It provides industry-specific market infrastructure and a full range of facilities for the gold & precious metals, diamonds & colored stones, energy and other commodities industries.

346 | DMCC is a free zone authority offering 100% business ownership, a guaranteed 50 year tax holiday and freehold property options.

347 | DMCC was rated 'A' by Standard and Poor's.

348 | "DMCC currently (March 2006) has over 720 registered free zone businesses in various commodity sectors, including gold and precious metals, diamonds and colored stones, tea and energy and I expect this to rise to 1,000 by the end of 2006."
Gaiti Rabbani, Chief Marketing Officer, *Dubai Multi Commodities Center (DMCC)*

349 | The Dubai Multi Commodities Center (DMCC) introduced in January 2006 Dubai Good Delivery (DGD) standard for silver bars. This standard, specifically designed for silver bars, fully complements the required international standards. DMCC has initially approved 7 international refiners for the DGD accreditation and more are expected.

350 | "DMCC has imposed strict laws and rules to control diamond trade through the UAE, along with the appliance of the Kimberly Process agreement that the UAE signed in 2003, which entails member countries to supervise and control their internal regulations related to diamond imports and exports."
Ahmed Bin Sulayem, Executive Director, *DMCC*

351 | "International standards and quality, along with best business practice are the guiding principles at DMCC, and we are continually seeking ways and means to improve the tradability of precious metals, by increasing confidence in the quality of bars, for local

Financial Markets

and regional markets. In extending Dubai Good Delivery (DGD) standard to silver, we aim to ensure that the quality of silver traded through Dubai will meet the highest international standards."
Colin Griffith, Executive Director, *Gold & Precious Metals at DMCC* and Chairman, *DGCX*

DDE |

352 | The Dubai Diamond Exchange (DDE) is the 1st diamond bourse within the Arab region, serving a broader region of growing trade flows beyond the Middle East. The Exchange facilitates the trade of rough and polished diamonds in and through the region. DDE was created by the Dubai Multi Commodities Center (DMCC), as part of its ongoing strategy to create an industry-specific market infrastructure.

353 | The DDE is a member of the World Federation of Diamond Bourses (WFDB), making it the first WFDB-affiliated bourse in the Arab world. Members of the Dubai Diamond Exchange (DDE) can directly access 25 other diamond bourses that are members of the World Federation.

354 | "Dubai Multi Commodities Center (DMCC) is proud to be associated with the World Diamond Council (WDC) and fully supports its aims. We are fully committed to the Kimberly Process and we have been instrumental in making the UAE the first Arab country to implement the Kimberley Process Certification Scheme (KPCS), as part of our endeavour to align the trade with global standards."
Dr. David Rutledge, Chief Executive Officer, *Dubai Multi Commodities Center (DMCC)*

355 | **The Diamond Tower** established by DGCX will host world diamond companies such as Christies, Rosy Blue, JAA, Eurostar, Love Diamond Company, Tashi Crystal Necklace, in addition to prominent regional firms such as Damas and Taiba.

356 | "In addition to it being the only diamond bourse in the Arab world and the only one in the region that is a member of the World Federation of Diamond bourses, the Dubai Diamond Exchange (DDE) manages an active rough diamond market. In 2005, approximately AED 242 million ($66 million) worth of rough diamonds was tendered at the diamond exchange. It is also the only exchange in the region with the mission of expanding and meeting the diamond trade from mining to manufacturing diamond jewelery."
Noora Jamsheer, CEO of Dubai Diamond Exchange, *Dubai Multi Commodities Center (DMCC)*

Financial Markets

DGC |

357 | The Dubai Gem Certification (DGC), the world's first to be ISO certified, is a unique service created to facilitate certification for and to provide advisory services in gemstones, pearls and jewelry items from globally recognized certification bodies.

358 | The DGC entered into partnership agreements with leading institutions from across the world to offer first class diamonds, gemstones, pearls and jewelry certificates such as the American Gem Society Laboratories (AGSL), the world-renowned Gubelin Gem Laboratory and Directorate of Precious Metals & Gem Stones Testing, Kingdom of Bahrain. These institutions boast the presence of leading gemologists as well as the trust of the global gems and jewelry trade.

359 | "The Dubai Gem Certification is an initiative to ensure that the gems and jewelery trade in the region is provided with the means to apply international standards in our markets. It will promote ethical and transparent trade practices and provide that competitive edge to regional businesses. The reputation of our members will be enhanced further as they will be seen to set and maintain the highest possible standards of business ethics and professionalism in the jewelry industry."
Tawfic Farah, Executive Director, *Diamonds and Coloured Stones, DMCC*

360 | "The DGC service will have a reputation for integrity in the business community and will at the same time build confidence amongst the buyers and the public in our gems and jewelry industry. We aim to be a standard of excellence that will bring us international esteem and recognition and will create a new benchmark in gem and jewelry certification."
Laurent Grenier de Cardenal, Director, *Coloured Stones & Gem Certification Services, DGC*

DTTC |

361 | "The Dubai Tea Trading Center (DTTC), another successful initiative of DMCC, has set an ambitious goal of doubling its trade volume in 2 years. Over the past 11 months [April 2005-March 2006] DTTC, designed as an organized hub for physical storage of multi origin teas for buyers in different parts of the world, has recorded 2.9 million kilos of tea trade. The target is to boost trading volume to 5 to 6 million kilos in 2 years."
Dr. David Rutledge, Chief Executive Officer, *DMCC*

Financial Markets

362 | Among several facilities, the Dubai Tea Trading Center (DTTC) offers 60 days free storage from the time the tea is cleared and unstuffed into the warehouse. There are preferential clearing rates for the DTTC members.

363 | Dubai is an emerging market hub for the global tea market and is further consolidating its position amongst the fastest and largest growing hubs for the transaction of multi origin tea. In 2005, 96.6 million kg of tea were transacted through Dubai and an additional 57 million kg were shipped through Dubai ports.

DGCX |

364 | Dubai Gold and Commodities Exchange (DGCX), the 1st commodities exchange in the Middle East, opened its membership in June 2005 and received an overwhelming response of more than 270 applications in less than 2 months. Moreover, the DGCX signed an agreement with the Chicago Board of Trade (CBoT), a 157-year-old institution and leading global derivative exchange. In 2006, the DGCX expects to launch the world's 1st exchange-traded steel futures contract.

365 | "We are located in a unique time zone as far as commodities exchanges are concerned. Once Tokyo closes, there is a time gap of more than 7 hours before London Metal Exchange (LME) opens. We fill this gap and this gives traders the opportunity to engage in uninterrupted trade. With our long trading hours, our traders will get arbitrage opportunities with all leading markets around the world."
Arshad Khan, Director, *Dubai Gold and Commodities Exchange (DGCX)*

366 | The physical trade for gold in Dubai was around 1.7 tonnes per day for February 2006, but market analysts expect the potential volume for futures contracts to be between 10 to 50 times greater than this amount.

367 | DGCX said that a total of 16,421 kg of gold futures contracts were traded in February against 6,475 kg in January - an increase of 154%, and up till March 2006, the total value of gold futures traded on DGCX since its inception (22 November 2005) stands at $517.48 million or 29,575 kg of gold futures contracts. This reflects the lively interest in gold as an investment class, and Dubai's ambition to be a center of the world gold trade.

368 | The average number of contracts traded per day increased from 260 in December 2005 to 360 in January 2006, 821 in February and 1,910 in March, an increase of 430% from January.

Financial Markets

369 | A total of 64,444 contracts of gold and silver futures were traded during April 2006 as against 43,945 contracts in March 2006, an increase of 47%. The traded volume in gold futures segment stood at 40,429 during the month whereas silver accounted for 24,015 traded contracts.

370 | DGCX launched silver trading in March 2006 and aims to achieve a target of 20,000 futures contracts per day by the end of 2006.

371 | DGCX received approval from the Emirates Securities and Commodities Authority to launch currency futures trading and is expected to introduce it in June 2006. It will initially trade futures contracts in 3 currencies euro-dollar, yen-dollar and sterling-dollar.

372 | "People worldwide are recognizing Dubai as a gold and jewelry center for the Middle East, the Indian sub-continent and even Africa. I believe that with the development of the Dubai Gold and Commodities Exchange (DGCX), it will become one of the most lucrative and busiest in the world."
Moaz Barakat, Managing Director for the Middle East, Turkey and Pakistan, *World Gold Council*

373 | **Man Financial Middle East**, a subsidiary of Man Financial, the brokerage division of Man Group and one of the world's leading providers of brokerage services, has been granted membership of DGCX as both a broker and a clearing member.

374 | "The year 2005 has been an important one for the hedge fund industry in the Middle East, particularly with the emergence of a new international financial center in the region. The DIFC appears to be a crucial step toward the creation of locally focused funds, while the continued institutionalization of the industry has brought it into the mainstream of asset management."
Antoine Massad, Chief Executive Officer, *Man Investments Middle East Limited*

375 | "Dubai stands a better chance than many other business centers of becoming a technology savvy global financial hub. Dubai has all the right ingredients. If the fully automated international financial exchanges in commodities, foreign exchange and global stocks can operate from a free economy with higher operating efficiency and savings, nothing will prevent global traders from doing business here."
Jignesh Shah, Vice Chairman, *DGCX*

Financial Markets

DME |

376 | The Dubai Mercantile Exchange (DME) is a joint venture between Dubai Energy, a subsidiary of Dubai Holding, and the New York Mercantile Exchange (NYMEX), the world's largest physical commodity exchange. It will be the region's 1st energy futures exchange. Initially, the DME plans to list, in the third quarter of 2006, three contracts: Middle-East based sour crude oil, fuel oil and gold.

377 | **Dubai Energy** will actively evaluate key oil and gas prospects alongside leading international companies and it will also screen potential equity investments in the broad energy sector.

378 | All trades executed on the Dubai Mercantile Exchange will be cleared through, and guaranteed by the NYMEX AA+ rated clearinghouse.

379 | The Dubai Mercantile Exchange is uniquely positioned to provide price transparency and market liquidity for crude oil from the world's foremost oil producing and exporting region.

380 | DME will be the 1st exchange to introduce the new trading hub concept on an electronic trading floor. This will effectively create an energy trading community on the floor of the Exchange, and will not only help to generate liquidity but will further provide the opportunity for international firms to relocate to the floor of the DME, bringing together experienced traders, global banks, local institutions and individuals from around the world.

381 | "No one tells you that it cannot be done, that it should not be done. The only pushback has always been let's do it bigger, let's do it better, and let's do it smarter."
Ahmed Sharaf, Chief Executive Officer, *Dubai Energy*

Financial Markets

5 3
1 3 5
3 5 4 1
1 3 5 5 4
3 2 1 1 6 4 6
4 8 9 7 0 1
1 5 5 4 0 5 4 5
0 5 5 4 6 5
3 5 4 7 6 0 4 4 6
6 7 9 8 0 2
1 6 1 1 6
5 6 5 0 1 2
6 8
6 5 1 5
8 7 1 0 1 7 8
3 5 4 0
5 4 0 3 5 4
0 6 4 4
0 7 5
0 6 5 7
2 1 2 0 1 3 5
1 3 5 4
0 3 5 7 5
0 3 5 4
1 5 6
7 8 1 3 1 0 5 4
4 1 5 6 4 0 3 4 5
0 3 5 4 7 8 0 3 3 5 3 5 0
0 3 4 3 5 2 8 7 3 2 2 3 1 0 3 4 6 5
1 6 5 5 4 4 5 4 6 5
0 3 4 1 0 5 6 1 6
0 6 5 4

BANKING & INSURANCE | 4

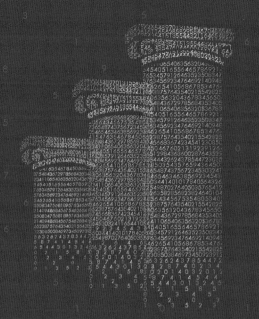

Banking and Insurance

Dubai has the most open, transparent and trustworthy banks in the region. Both Dubai and UAE banks generally held advanced rankings on the list of the best 100 Arab banks, published by "Euromoney". Around 50% of Dubai and UAE banks' net profits was a result of an increase in real estate financing and investment portfolio management in capital markets. Dubai also houses 50% of the insurance companies in the UAE. And as the country's insurance sector opens up, more international insurers will be looking to set up here. To do so, they will have to be backed by an 'A' rating from an international credit rating agency.

"It's pretty clear to us that from a long-term perspective, the phenomenon of Dubai is real. We might have debates around absolute valuations at any given point of time, which is what people do when they are picking stocks. But in terms of the long term I think we are fairly comfortable with Dubai as an economy that will be a significant factor in the region as well as globally. This is why we are putting significant resources here."

William Mills, Chairman and Chief Executive Officer of Corporate and Investment Banking (EMEA), *Citigroup*

OVERVIEW |

382 | "Emirates banks are the most open banks in the region."
Standard and Poor's

383 | Dubai is leading the way in the Middle East in attracting international investment banks wanting to establish a presence in the region. High liquidity, coupled with high oil and gas prices, are boosting the demand for financial services especially advisory work, such as merger and acquisition.

384 | The **UAE Central Bank** has set a minimum capital adequacy ratio of 10%.

385 | During the year 2005, the banking sector witnessed distinguished performance due to the significant rise in national income, besides the unprecedented upturns in various economic sectors such as construction, real-estate, tourism, trade and aviation. All these sectors depended basically on the banking sector to finance their activities.
Emirates Banks Association Annual Report 2005

386 | "The outlook for the coming period looks extremely positive. With higher oil prices now stabilized, we can expect a continuing high level of investment in construction and infrastructure projects as well as robust growth in other sectors. Although 2006 may not achieve the stellar growth of last year, we believe it will be extremely healthy."
Abdul Aziz Al-Ghurair, CEO, *Mashreqbank* and Director, *Abdulla Al Ghurair Group*

Banking & Insurance

387 | Dubai and UAE banks held advanced rankings on the list of the best 100 Arab banks, published by "Euromoney" magazine in December 2005. Emirates Bank International ranked 10th, while Mashreqbank ranked 14th, Abu Dhabi Commercial Bank ranked 17th, Dubai Islamic Bank climbed up from the 37th position to rank 27th. Commercial Bank of Dubai ranked 37th while the First Gulf Bank jumped from the 65th position to rank 43rd.

388 | A new UAE banking law is expected in 2006, with a background of pending implementation of revised Basel II Accord recommendations.

389 | It is expected that the Free Trade Agreement (FTA) between the UAE and the US will lure US banks into the UAE market once the banking sector is liberalized given that in the last 5 years the UAE banks' profitability has exceeded the US banks' profitability. Consistently high ratios of return on assets and return on equity, along with a high ratio of non-performing loans, will make the UAE banking sector more attractive to US banks. The latter would seek to enter the UAE market to enjoy high profits and to capitalize on improving non-performing loans by using modern management and exploiting untouched opportunities in diverse economic sectors.

390 | In early 2006, there were 46 active banks in the UAE, 21 national banks and 25 foreign banks. The branches of these banks increased to 564, including 449 branches for national banks and 115 branches for foreign banks.

391 | At the moment, all banking activity in Dubai is regulated by the UAE Central Bank. It places many restrictions on foreign banks such as they may have no more than 8 branches in the UAE, and every commercial bank operating in Dubai must have paid up capital available amounting to at least AED 40 million

392 | Many of the world's largest banks already have significant presence in Dubai, big names such as Banque Paribas, HSBC, ABN Amro, Citibank, Barclays, Dresdner, Lloyds and Merrill Lynch all already have offices in the Emirate, and when the DIFC is completed, it is expected to house even more offshore branches of the world's major banks.

393 | The Central Bank Law establishes 5 principal categories of institutions in the UAE - commercial banks, investment banks, financial establishments, financial intermediaries, and monetary intermediaries - all of which must be licensed by both the Central Bank and the local licensing authorities.

Banking & Insurance

MARKET PERFORMANCE |

394 | According to the UAE Central Bank, the money supply on the local market rose by 29.9% from AED 80.8 billion ($22 billion) by the end of 2004 to AED 104.4 billion by the end of 2005. The local liquidity rose in the market by 33.8% from AED 242.2 billion to AED 324.1 billion while the total local liquidity in the broad sense of the word rose by 36.5% from AED 304.2 billion to AED 415.4 billion.

395 | UAE Banks' profits increased at exceptional speed, with 8 banks, all local, breaking the AED 1 billion level. Additionally, 2 of these banks (National Bank of Abu Dhabi, with AED 2.58 billion and Mashreqbank, with AED 2.01 billion) went on to crack the AED 2 billion mark.

396 | The substantial growth in interest income from IPO financing, coupled with other non-interest income from capital gains and brokerage fee income, have been one of the main driving force behind strong growth in Dubai and UAE banks' profits during 2005.

397 | "50% of Dubai and UAE banks' net profits result from enlargement in real estate funding or investment portfolio management in capital markets, while the remaining percentage results from banking services."
Mohamed Ali Yassine, General Manager, *Emirates Islamic Shares & Bonds Center*

398 | "The region is investing heavily in new infrastructure with project financing in the region totaling $44.3 billion last year (2005). Dubai is a prime example, with its huge investments in real estate and transport infrastructure. With the strong sovereign support and the expected high oil prices, the outlook for project finance is positive."
Jan Willem Plantagie, Credit Analyst, *Standard & Poor's*

399 | "We have been concocting major investments to expand our presence in Dubai. During the past 12 months we hired more than 500 new personnel in Dubai and we are keen on rendering it our Middle East operations hub."
David Hodgkinson, Deputy Chairman and CEO, *HSBC Bank Middle East*

400 | The number of banks offering e-banking in the UAE has risen steadily since the service was first launched in 1996, with 16 out of 46 commercial banks now providing e-banking services to their clients.

Banking & Insurance

401 | "With so many more deals, the frequency of travel has increased. There reaches a critical point at which it becomes more effective to just stay in Dubai."
Omar Al-Salehi, Head of Middle East Investment Banking, *UBS*

402 | Across Asia, bankers claim that the emergence of Dubai as a financial center with global linkages has helped improve the comfort level among bankers and fund managers seeking to build bridges with the oil-rich Middle East.

403 | "The UAE economy has rapidly evolved from a youthful economy to one that is now showing signs of maturity. At present, oil production is running close to full capacity, the loan-to-stable resources ratio in the banking system is approaching its statutory limits, housing rents are becoming comparable to those in Europe and the US, and equity prices have more than kept pace with the rise in net earnings."
Hany Genena, Senior Economist, *EFG-Hermes*

404 | According to Fitch Ratings, UAE banks are not facing any systemic risk from the recent crash of local and regional stock markets.

405 | Credit card holders in the UAE grew from 1 to 4 million, ballooning 400% in the last 3 years, according to the Emirates Banks Association Annual Report 2005.

406 | "Combining cash with the search for new investment opportunities, many affluent investors are positioning themselves to use Dubai as an increasingly important point of origin – a base from which to establish new links with eastern Asia."
The Banker Magazine

407 | The UAE's Anti Money Laundering and Suspicious Cases Unit (AMLSCU) and Serious Organized Crime Agency (SOCA) of UK have signed a MoU for mutual cooperation in different areas including exchange of financial information related to money laundering and terrorist financing.

408 | Dubai authorities acted to keep tighter control over money flows through Dubai. The government tracks withdrawals of cash above a low threshold and requires banks to investigate their customers before opening accounts and report suspicious transactions in line with standards set by the United Nations and the Organization for Economic Co-operation and Development (OECD).

409 | By year-end 2005, the Central Bank of the UAE signed an Advisory Agreement with the

Banking & Insurance

International Finance Corporation (IFC), the private sector arm of the World Bank, to support corporate governance reforms in the UAE's banking sector.

410 | UAE banks reported 29.83% Emiratization by the end of 2005 in comparison to 9.83% reported in 1987 and up 2.21% from 2004. The figures from Emirates Banks Association annual report 2005 show that the number of national employees increased by 1,560 to reach a total of 6,957 in 2005 as against 5,397 nationals in 2004.

411 | **Shuaa Capital**, the leading UAE investment bank, announced its audited 12 months profits of AED 362 million ($98.6 million) for the year ended 31 March 2006 versus AED 224 million in the comparative year, a strong increase of 62%. Total consolidated revenues were up by 73% from last year to a record AED 502 million.

ASSETS & LOANS |

412 | The total assets of banks operating in the UAE according to the syndicated budget of banks rose from AED 449.7 billion by the end of 2004 to AED 638 billion ($173.8 billion) by the end of 2005, up by 42%.

413 | The assets of national banks rose from AED 344.1 billion to AED 499.1 billion ($136 billion) up by 45% while the credit facilities provided by the banks to customers rose from AED 190.7 billion to AED 280.6 billion and local investments from AED 7.9 billion to AED 16.9 billion.

414 | The assets of foreign banks increased from AED 105.7 billion by the end of 2004 to AED 138.9 billion ($37.8 billion) by the end of 2005, up by 31.4% while the credit facilities provided by these banks to their customers rose from AED 56.3 billion to AED 72.5 billion and their local investments from AED 2.1 billion to AED 2.22 billion

415 | By the end of the first quarter of 2006, the total assets of national banks grew by 55.7% to AED 750 billion compared with AED 481.3 billion for the corresponding period last year. In this connection, high-ranking banking sources emphasised that the profits of national banks would continue this year. The profits grew by 75.4% to AED 4.7 billion compared with AED 2.67 billon for the corresponding period last year.

416 | The volume of loans and facilities granted by national banks registered a remarkable growth that stood at 41.7% last year to reach AED 312.8 billion at the end of 2005, compared to AED 220.7 billion at the end of 2004.

Banking & Insurance

417 | The average customer deposits (including inter-bank lending) for national banks exceeded 45.3% in 2005 reaching AED 337.3 billion ($92 billion), well above the previous year's figure of AED 232.1 billion, in an environment of a fast-growing economy and rising interest rates.

418 | According to Central Bank of the UAE statistics, the value of personal loans granted by banks operating in the country increased 13% to AED 97.7 billion ($26.6 billion) in 2005 compared to AED 59.6 billion by the end of 2004. This included AED 70.5 billion reserved for personal loans for commercial purposes and AED 27.3 billion reserved for personal loans for consumption purposes, by the end of 2005.

419 | "Apart from growth in credit cards, there has also been growth in the personal loans business because of the rise in population, availability of goods and services and the purchasing power of the Dirham."
Raymond O-Neil, Managing Director, *HSBC Middle East Finance Company*

NATIONAL BANKS |

420 | The **National Bank of Dubai** (NBD) is the largest bank in Dubai and the 2nd largest overall in the UAE, enjoying a market share of around 13% and 6% of total customer deposits and loans respectively. The bank operates a network of over 30 branches in the UAE, with the majority located in Dubai.

421 | National Bank of Dubai achieved net profits for the year 2005 reaching AED 1.103 billion ($300 million) which represents a growth of 18.9% (AED 175 million) over year 2004. The bank's balance sheet for 2005 stands at AED 51.4 billion ($14 billion) which represents a growth of 27.7% (AED 11.1 billion) over 2004 level of AED 40.3 billion. The bank's balance sheet has grown by 82% in the last 5 years. Despite growth of the loan portfolio the capital adequacy ratio stands at 18.3% as at the end of 2005.

422 | In 2005, National Bank of Dubai was awarded international credit ratings of 'A1' by Moody's and 'A' by Standard & Poor's. In their analysis of the bank, Moody's drew attention to the Bank's credit strengths whereas Standard & Poor's rated the bank's strong capitalization, low risk profile and superior asset quality and liquidity.

423 | The Private Office, National Bank of Dubai's private banking service, has been named the Best Private Bank in the UAE by the leading International magazine, Euromoney.

Banking & Insurance

424 | At the end of 2005, **Commercial Bank of Dubai** reported a record net profit of AED 551 million, with a return on equity of 19.5% and total assets of AED 15.28 billion.

425 | In 2005, **Mashreqbank** achieved a record net profit of AED 1.739 billion ($474 million), an increase of 131% over its profit of AED 751 million in 2004. The Group's operating income for 2005 jumped 80% to reach AED 3.106 billion. Shareholders' equity increased by 50% to AED 7.26 billion, outpacing the growth in assets and improving the bank's equity to asset ratio to 15.8%.

426 | The **Emirates Bank Group** (EBG) recorded a net profit of AED 1.732 billion ($472 million) for 2005. This represents an increase of 78% over the AED 972.1 million earned in 2004.

427 | **Dubai Bank** will continue to expand its operations and venture into new business areas capitalizing on key value driven opportunities during 2006. This includes launching a brokerage company, which will offer a highly secure online trading facility, as well as other new products and services.

428 | "Our return on equity (ROE) for the year 2005 was 21% and our growth over the 1st half results, in terms of net profit, is 121%. After only 3 years in operation, this is truly a great achievement by the team and a testimony to a thriving regional economy, paired with various international select deals that we had the fortune of participating in."
Ziad Makkawi, Former Chief Executive Officer, *Dubai Bank*

429 | Dubai Bank has announced a net profit of AED 102.8 million ($28 million) for 2005. The Bank reported a 97% growth in its total assets, reaching AED 4.8 billion ($1.3 billion) in 2005 compared to AED 2.4 billion in 2004. Deposits increased to AED 3.7 billion and loans and advances to AED 1.6 billion, representing an increase of 94.5% and 37% respectively, over the previous year.

430 | The UAE has the third largest mutual fund industry in the GCC totaling $12 billion with potential to grow to $50 billion by 2010.

431 | "The UAE's investment management industry has the huge potential of growing up to $50 billion by 2010 and it will be the fastest growing industry in the GCC."
Haissam Arabi, Managing Director, *Shuaa Capital*

432 | "Banks in the UAE have enough liquidity and a will strong enough to perform this role

Banking & Insurance

(in project financing) in an exemplary manner and be pioneers for the whole world. National banks can finance these projects either individually or through forming consortium lending."

Saleh Salem Bin Omeir Al Shamsi, Chairman, *Abu Dhabi Chamber of Commerce and Industry*

INSURANCE |

433 | Dubai is considered the hub of the insurance industry in the UAE. It hosts 49% of the total number of insurance companies, followed by Abu Dhabi with 33% and Sharjah 10.4%.

434 | The UAE's insurance sector is expected to double by 2010 and a significant part of the market's annual 15% growth will be driven by the exponential increase of the region's logistics industry.

435 | The insurance market in Dubai is one of the most attractive in the region. This is due mainly to the high economic growth rates in the market.

436 | The results of a survey conducted by DCCI among the insurance companies in Dubai to assess the expected impact of the current Free Trade Agreements (FTAs) showed that insurance companies are optimistic about the expected FTAs in terms of increasing the competition and improving the services provided by the sector. They expect it will open new areas and opportunities to improve business and decrease risks, extend the scope of e-commerce and develop new ways of marketing channels.

437 | "As the UAE opens up the insurance sector, international insurers are looking to enter it. This will increase job opportunities, intensify competition and bring new products and services and help the UAE insurance industry to mature. Local companies, however, are firmly established and strong enough to weather the change."
Sheikh Faisal Bin Khalid Al Qassemi, Chairman, *Emirates Insurance Association*

438 | One of the insurance industry's biggest revenue providers is logistics, due to its highly diverse requirements including the shipment of goods, storage and warehousing of commodities and perishables, fire and flooding building insurance and staff medical policies.

439 | The insurance sector in Dubai and the UAE is expected to increase remarkably along

Banking & Insurance

with its demand for new employees, according to the Emirates Insurance Association, an umbrella organization for 44 insurance companies operating in the country.

440 | "The insurance sector in the UAE represents 19% of the financial services market and 1.5% of the GDP. The saving ratio in the country is high, reaching 31%. The insurance premiums quota does not exceed 5% of these savings. Insurance companies' share yield reaches 11%, against 8.9% on real estate companies' shares."
Foutouh Al Zayani, Former Insurance and Re-insurance Manager, *DIFC*

441 | Among the UAE insurance companies, 12% are small, 43% are medium small, 15% are medium large and 30% are large.

442 | For Dubai National Insurance and Reinsurance Company, the financial year 2005 was a year of success achieving net profits of AED 305.76 million ($83.3 million) up from only AED 80.40 million in 2004 (an increase of 280%).

443 | Experts and analysts expected the continued growth and good performance of the insurance sector during 2006, similar to the strong results achieved by companies in 2005. The profits of some insurance companies skyrocketed, reaching **300%** in such cases as Oman Insurance company.

444 | "The accelerating economic growth in the UAE and those witnessed by different economic sectors gives very optimistic indicators for the insurance sector in 2006. I expect that the growth in the volume of subscribed installments will range between 12% and 18% over the year, with continued growth of real-estate activities, the introduction of new products to the insurance sector, as well as demographic growth."
Abdel Muttalib Mustafa, General Manager, *Oman Insurance Company*

445 | 22 insurance companies listed in the local financial markets scored net profits of AED 3.5 billion ($953 million) during 2005, while the shareholders' rights increased to AED 12 billion ($3.27 billion).

446 | "Initial forecasts suggest that well over 20,000 insurance professionals will be working at the DIFC within a matter of years and there is a real need for the respected, authoritative qualifications that the Chartered Insurance Institute (CII) provides."
Dr. Alexander Scott, Director General, *Chartered Insurance Institute (CII)*

Banking & Insurance

ISLAMIC FINANCE | **5**

Islamic Finance

Dubai is the regional hub for Islamic banking and finance and it is quickly becoming the preferred means of finance. Islamic financing in the UAE is increasing at an annual rate of 30%. In 2005, Dubai managed the world's largest ever sukuk and it is set to become the world's largest sukuk market.

Takaful, the Islamic alternative to insurance, is predicted to grow steadily. Industry forecasts estimate that the global Takaful personal insurance sector, including Health Takaful, will reach around $5 billion by 2015, with the UAE expected to generate 10% of this figure.

"During the past 30 years, Islamic banks have emerged across the world. Today there are more than 280 Islamic banks in 48 countries with deposits approaching $400 billion. Added to that, about 300 traditional banks have established Islamic subsidiaries or offer Islamic products."
HE Dr. Mohamed Khalfan Bin Kharbash, Minister of Finance and Industry and Chairman, *Dubai Islamic Bank*

OVERVIEW |

447 | Dubai's Islamic Finance landscape is changing rapidly. In the next 3 to 5 years, there is an expected establishment of new fully-fledged Islamic banks and companies, and a wholesale conversion of some conventional banks into Islamic ones as well as Islamic product offerings by many conventional banks.

448 | The McKinsey 2005-2006 Competitiveness Report published by the World Islamic Banking Conference declared that the growth rate of Islamic banks in the UAE is estimated at 11%.

449 | "The Islamic finance and Takaful industry are booming in the Far East and GCC countries. And, because of the strategic vision of the local authorities and their dynamism, Dubai will attract more new investors looking for Shariah compliant instruments and solutions."
Chakib Abouzaid, Chief Executive Officer, *Takaful Re*

450 | Two growth signs of the local Islamic financial industry can be observed in Dubai and the UAE, especially after the prompt growth in the number of Islamic banks, which doubled in 2004 (according to Meed Magazine). First, is the move by local banks towards becoming fully Shariah-compliant - in spite of the enormously complicated task of restructuring balance sheets and product offerings - or at least to create an Islamic arm. Second, is the growing capabilities of existing institutions, in the use of the Islamic structures in local project finance and debt capital market transactions.

Islamic Finance

451 | "Hotels are suited to Islamic finance structures because the revenue stream is generated from the value of the asset. All products are asset-backed and lend themselves to this model."
Ashruff Jamall, Partner, *PricewaterhouseCoopers Dubai*

452 | The UAE was elected in June 2005 to preside over the Board of Trustees of the International Islamic Commercial and Arbitration Center (IICAC), for the next 3 years.

453 | The secret behind the longing to join the Islamic bandwagon lies in the immense success of the existing Islamic banks in the UAE. The 4 Dubai and UAE Islamic banks, Dubai Islamic Bank, Sharjah Islamic Bank, Abu Dhabi Islamic Bank and Emirates Islamic Bank, displayed a remarkable performance during 2005 with a 116% increase in their net profits at the end of the third quarter to AED 1.86 billion ($507 million).

454 | "We plan to open 10 more branches this year in different parts of the UAE, so we will have 21 branches by end of 2006. We expect profits to grow higher this year with new initiatives that will be launched. Emirates Islamic Bank's (EIB) assets doubled to AED 4.8 billion in 2005 in comparison with the previous year."
Faisal Aqil, General Manager, Retail, *Emirates Islamic Bank*

455 | The growth of Islamic retail deposits in Dubai is expected to increase by 29% between 2004 and 2008, and retail credit is set to rise by 16% annually. Islamic banks' share of retail deposits in all UAE banks increased to 14% at the end of 2004, compared to 10% in 2001, which is attributed to the wide acceptance of Islamic retail banking in the UAE. Their share of retail credit rose to 11% at the end of 2004.

DIB |

456 | Dubai Islamic Bank (DIB) has the unique distinction of being the world's 1st fully-fledged Islamic bank. Since its formation in 1975, it has been a pioneering institution that combines the best of traditional Islamic values with the technology and innovation that characterize the best of modern banking.

457 | Dubai Islamic Bank has a leading role in making Dubai and the UAE a regional and global hub for banking services, particularly Islamic. The total amount of Islamic banking operations managed and lead by the bank has exceeded AED 100 billion ($27 billion) over the past 2 years.

Islamic Finance

458 | "Dubai Islamic Bank achieved outstanding results for the fiscal year 2005, recording AED 1.06 billion of net profit. The year was marked by large financial transactions lead-managed by the bank, and by an expansion plan covering regional and international markets. The year 2005 was a milestone in the history of Dubai Islamic Bank, which celebrated its 30th anniversary."
HE Dr. Mohamed Khalfan Bin Kharbash, UAE Minister of State for Finance and Industry and Chairman, *Dubai Islamic Bank (DIB)*

459 | Dubai Islamic Bank recorded a 127% increase in its first quarter profit of 2006 to AED 695 million compared to AED 305 million in the corresponding period of 2005. The Bank's total assets grew by a record of 109% to AED 63.4 billion ($17 billion) at the end of the first quarter 2006, up from AED 30.3 billion by the end of first quarter 2005.

TAKAFUL |

460 | The Dubai International Financial Center (DIFC) is committed to actively promoting the growth and development of the Islamic alternative to insurance (Takaful) industry in accordance with Shariah principles. The Takaful market is one of the fastest growing in the world. It is expected to grow at nearly 20% per annum to reach $7.4 billion in global annual premiums in 15 years.

461 | With an authorised capital of $500 million and paid-up capital of $125 million, **Takaful Re** has plans to focus on re-takaful business in the MENA and Islamic countries. Takaful Re is dedicated to offer Shariah compliant reinsurance and related services to the growing Takaful and Islamic insurance markets. Takaful Re will offer reinsurance capacity in all major lines of property, marine and family re-takaful business.

462 | Takaful Re, one of the most financially secure re-Takaful companies in the Middle East & North Africa (MENA) region, has been licensed by Dubai Financial Services Authority (DFSA) to operate from the Dubai International Financial Center (DIFC).

463 | "Apart from ARIG, our shareholders are the most prestigious financial institutions in UAE and the GCC countries. Dubai for Takaful Re is the best place to be as a reinsurer."
Chakib Abouzaid, Chief Executive Officer, *Takaful Re*

464 | **Salama** Islamic Arab Insurance Company, the world's largest Takaful and Re-Takaful company has announced a provisional 2005 net profit of AED 110 million ($30 million).

Islamic Finance

up from AED 3.599 million ($1 million) in 2004, an increase of approximately 3000%.

465 | "We fully expect this strong growth in profitability will continue in 2006 and beyond, driven by a very aggressive expansion into new markets and products. We are investing close to AED 1 billion ($272 million) in growing the company and are confident net profits will be higher in the coming years. We expect them to quadruple by 2010."
Sheikh Khalid Bin Zayed Bin Saqr Al Nehayan, Chairman, *Salama*

466 | Salama Islamic Arab Insurance Company has concluded a landmark agreement to establish a Shariah syndicate at Lloyd's of London, the 1st of its kind at the world's premier insurance market.

467 | "Health Takaful, along with Life Takaful, will make a significant contribution to our growth over the next five years. Industry forecasts predict that the global Takaful personal insurance sector, including Health Takaful, will reach AED 17.8 billion ($4.8 billion) by 2015. Saudi Arabia is expected to generate close to AED 3.3 billion, followed by the UAE with AED 1.75 billion and Egypt AED 1.7 billion."
Dr. Saleh Malaikah, Vice Chairman and CEO, *Salama*

468 | Dubai Islamic Insurance and Reinsurance **(AMAN)** net profits for 2005 rose by 865% to reach AED 82.04 million ($22 million) from AED 8.5 million ($2.3 million) in 2004. Its stock earnings increased by 112%. The value of insurance premiums paid increased by 77.5% in 2005 to reach $25 million. The company's assets grew by 134% to $67 million in 2005 compared to $28.6 million in 2004.

469 | "AMAN achieved excellent results last year and we have decided to distribute15% of the profits and an extra 15% bonus shares to the shareholders. We will also apply a recommendation to the General Assembly to raise AMAN capital into AED 200 million ($54.5 million)."
HE Sultan Bin Saeed Al Mansouri, Chairman of the Board of Directors, *AMAN*

470 | "Our impressive financial results for the year 2005 has stemmed from our significant achievements during the year, primarily in our trendsetting role of developing the Islamic Takaful Insurance sector in catering to a diverse range of customers. Our strategy has always been to offer innovative market-driven Islamic insurance products and services and this is truly reflected in our performance."
Hussain Al Meeza, Managing Director, *AMAN*

Islamic Finance

471 | Swiss Reinsurance Company **(Swiss Re)**, the world's biggest reinsurer by market value, launched its first Islamic product in Dubai aiming to grab a share of a small but rapidly growing market globally.

472 | "Islamic insurance is a few years behind the Islamic banking industry but we do see the beginnings of a burgeoning market."
Chris Singleton, Head of life and health business for the Middle East and South Asia, *Swiss Re*

473 | "Change is taking place fast in the UAE market and in the region with people increasingly becoming aware of pensions, health and life insurance. We foresee an explosion in life insurance and savings and hence we are preparing to grab our share."
Oussama Al Kaissi, General Manager, *Abu Dhabi National Takaful Company (ADNTC)*

ISLAMIC FINANCE |

474 | The Dubai International Financial Center (DIFC) has set up a strategic Islamic Finance Advisory Council comprising key industry personalities to jointly work with it on matters relating to the development of Islamic finance. The new council will play a key role in providing strategic advice on Islamic finance and help in the development of the industry, in general, and within DIFC, in particular.

475 | Financial Times Stock Exchange **(FTSE)** Group and Dubai International Financial Exchange (DIFX) have signed an agreement to develop a range of conventional and Shariah compliant equity indices. These indices are intended to become chosen benchmarks for the performance of all significant regional markets including the DIFX and specific markets of interest to DIFX participants. FTSE and the DIFX will work together to create a family of indices suitable for the creation of financial products, such as index funds, warrants, certificates and Exchange Traded Funds.

476 | A study indicates that the total Islamic financing in Dubai and the UAE is increasing at an annual rate of 30%. Apart from a few banks, which applied for fully-fledged Islamic finance companies, there are other local banks planning to offer Islamic products through special Islamic windows.

477 | The **Dubai Department of Civil Aviation (DCA)** issued a $1 billion 3 year Ijarah facility (Islamic-compliant leasing agreement) aiming to partially fund the development and expansion of Dubai International Airport.

Islamic Finance

SUKUK |

478 | Dubai's **Ports, Customs and Free Zone Corporation (PCFC)** listed its $3.5 billion sukuk on Dubai International Financial Exchange (DIFX), hoping to give the world's biggest Islamic bond greater visibility after a hugely successful issue. The sukuk, the 1st convertible instrument in the Islamic finance market and one of the 10 largest convertible offerings ever, was managed by Dubai Islamic Bank and Barclays Capital. The sukuk, originally meant to raise $2.8 billion, received more than $11 billion in orders and was scaled up to $3.5 billion.

479 | "DIB has broken its own previously held record of lead managing the world's largest ever Sukuk. Building on previous successful Sukuk issues over the past year, DIB has further strengthened its position as the world's number one arranger of Sukuk."
Saad Abdul Razak, Chief Executive Officer, *DIB*

480 | **National Bonds Corporation (NBC)** announced that more than AED 130 million worth of National Bonds have been sold in the 1st month of sales. The unique Shariah compliant saving scheme, which was made available to the public in March 2006, has received a staggering 50,000 applicants during the 1st month of sales. The company, equally owned by Dubai Holding, Emaar Properties and Dubai Bank, said its National Bonds scheme was patterned along similar programs in Ireland, New Zealand and the UK, where funds raised from Premium Bonds exceed $37.8 billion.

481 | "Without doubt, Dubai has been a vanguard in successfully adopting the instrument of sukuk as a means of tapping the needed liquidity for its various projects. Sukuks launched with the direct or indirect involvement of the Government of Dubai include Nakheel sukuk, Dubai Civil Aviation (DCA) sukuk, Dubai Multi Commodities Center (DMCC) sukuk, Emirates sukuk and the PCFC sukuk. The aggregate value of these sukuks is an enormous $5.6 billion. This amount is about half the value of all sukuks launched globally so far."
Sohain Zubairi, Vice President and Head of Shariah Structuring, Documentation and Product Development, *DIB*

482 | Dubai is the capital of the sukuk industry, which has shown tremendous growth on a global level in the past 5 years, rising from $100 million to around $12.5 billion.

Islamic Finance

AMLAK |

483 | Amlak Finance, in which Emaar Properties holds a 45% stake, has proved to be one of the most innovative and far-sighted operators in the market. Amlak's 2005 growth has been boosted by a number of high profile expansions and developments, including the raising of a $200 million Sukuk, a $75 million real estate fund, and a well-received one-for-one rights issue that increased the company's capital to AED 1.5 billion to become the largest publicly held Islamic finance company in the UAE.

484 | Amlak Finance performed annual profits of AED 106 million (after depositor's share), based on the latest management accounts in 2005. The 122% rise represents an increase from the 2004 figure of AED 48 million. The profit before the depositor's share was AED 193.5 million, an increase of 233% more than the previous year.

485 | "Dubai is the ideal regional hub for Islamic banking and finance industry. The sukuk issues will open up significant opportunities to accommodate a wider base of investors, both Muslim and non-Muslim, thus opposing conventional instruments that lose out on Islamic liquidity."
Mohammed Ali Al Hashimi, Chief Executive Officer, *Amlak Finance*

TAMWEEL |

486 | Tamweel is a joint venture between two great organizations, Dubai Islamic Bank and the Ports, Customs and Free Zone Corporation (PCFC). It focuses solely on home financing for property that is ready to move into or property that is under construction.

487 | Tamweel announced the closure of its IPO with it being oversubscribed 500 times. The IPO which looked to raise AED 550 million worth of shares, saw 140,000 investors from across the region with a total amount in excess of AED 275 billion ($75 billion) collected in less than two weeks.

488 | "We believe the commitments to the Tamweel IPO result not only from the strong performance of Tamweel, but also show that investors recognize that Tamweel has a particular competitive advantage in the home loan industry."
Adel Al Shirawi, Chief Executive Officer, *Tamweel*

Islamic Finance

TRAVEL & TOURISM | 6

Travel & Tourism

Dubai... a haven for tourism. This Emirate expects 15 million tourists and 120 passengers by 2010, all of whom can be flown in on Emirates Airline, voted the best carrier in the Middle East and Africa for the past 3 years. Visitors will land in one of the world's top airports, the Dubai International Airport, which includes world-class duty free shopping. It is also predicted that 20,000 to 25,000 new hotel rooms and suites will be built by 2010, in addition to the 30,000 rooms currently available. In Dubai, there is plenty to do, whether you wish to indulge in year-round skiing, go on desert safaris or enjoy the Dubai Shopping Festival and Dubai Summer Surprises.

"We want to become number 1. Nobody cares about number 2."
HH Sheikh Ahmed Bin Saeed Al Maktoum, Chairman & Chief Executive, *Emirates Airline Group*

OVERVIEW |

489 | Tourism growth in Dubai touched 12% in 2005.

490 | The Dubai hospitality industry is anticipated to achieve an average annual growth rate of 7 to 10% over the next 5 to 10 years, and remain the best performer in the region.

491 | "Dubai provides an excellent standard of living in the region, with unparalleled educational and recreational facilities for individuals and families."
Obaid Humaid Al Tayer, Chairman, Dubai Chamber of Commerce and Industry (DCCI)

492 | "Dubai has become one of the most profitable locations globally for the hotel business. Our guests are not just interested in beach tourism, but in the city as well. There is a buzz about it, similar to that of New York."
Gerald Lawless, Chief Executive Officer, *Jumeirah Group*

493 | According to the Dubai Naturalization and Residency Department (DNRD), more than 30,000 travel and work visas are issued by Dubai every day. The department handles a staggering 100,000 transactions a day. That includes 50,000 passport entry and exit stamps at Dubai Airport as well as 20,000 at land borders and seaports.

494 | "Around 15,000 entry visas per day for tourism, work, mission and residency are issued per day over the internet."
Major Salah Bin Saloum, Deputy Director, *Office of entry visas*

495 | Dubai Naturalization and Immigration Department launched the "immediate visa" service which allows visitors to get an entry visa in less than one hour.

EMIRATES AIRLINE |

496 | Completing 20 years of operations in October 2005, Emirates Airline schedules close to 200 flights a day, an average of one flight taking off or landing every 8 minutes.

497 | Emirates Airline makes up more than 50% of the Dubai International Airport activities, and plans to raise this figure to 70% by 2010.

498 | Emirates Airline operates to 80 destinations in 55 countries with a fleet of 88 aircrafts. Alone, the airline operates 91 flights to UK and 49 to Germany weekly.

499 | One of the key highlights for Emirates Airline in 2005 was the company's signing of a massive $9.7 billion contract for 42 Boeing 777 aircraft at the 2005 Air Show. This brought the value of Emirates Airline's total order book for new aircraft to $33 billion.

500 | "If we take Emirates Airline's direct contribution to Dubai's economy, it is estimated to be $1.5 billion. When you take into account all the people we bring in, it is at least $5 billion."
HH Sheikh Ahmed Bin Saeed Al-Maktoum, Chairman & Chief Executive, *Emirates Airline Group*

501 | "The volume of operations of Emirates Airline will double by 2012. The fleet will be made up of 160 aircraft by 2015, with an option to add 50 more planes during that period so that the total number of planes would reach 210. The airline will fly 38 million passengers to 130 destinations by 2015."
Ghaith Al-Ghaith, Executive Vice President for Commercial Operations, *Emirates Airline*

502 | Determined to become the largest airline company in the world, Emirates Group employs over 26,000 people from 110 countries, including over 1,000 pilots from 90 countries and some 5,600 flight attendants from over 100 nationalities.

503 | Upon completion next year, Emirates Airline's engineering center will be one of the world's biggest civil aviation maintenance facilities, with 8 hangars fully equipped to handle heavy and light maintenance for the airline's entire fleet.

504 | Emirates Airline's net profits registered AED 2.8 billion ($762 million) for the fiscal year 2005-2006, representing a growth of 5% from the previous year. The airline's revenues reached AED 5.2 billion ($1.4 billion) during the same period, an increase of 27% from the previous year.

Travel & Tourism

505 | Emirates Airline, unlike most airlines, has posted profits for 17 years in a row, and returns of over $100 million a year to shareholders in dividends.

506 | Emirates Group has expressed its will to plunge into the mainstream hospitality industry, explaining that it is building a new large scale 5-star luxury hotel in Dubai. The $218 million, 70-storey, 350 meter-high building on Sheikh Zayed Road will rank among the world's 5 tallest hotels, and one of the largest in the UAE.

507 | Emirates Group has unveiled plans for the construction of the Emirates Marina Apartments project, estimated to cost AED 300 million ($81.7 million). The project is expected to be ready by September 2006.

508 | Emirates Airline was the 1st carrier in the region to offer online check-in services.

509 | Operational costs of Emirates Airline are 30% less than those of international carriers of a greater average volume of operations. Annual profits doubled every 3.5 years in the first 11 years, and doubled once every 4 years.

510 | Emirates Airline has won more than 270 world awards and was recently voted the best carrier in the Middle East and Africa for the 3rd consecutive year.

511 | The average seat occupancy of Emirates Airline has increased to 74.6% in 2005, against 73.4% in 2004.

512 | Emirates Airline's productivity is 66% higher than the average productivity of other International Air Transport Association (IATA) members. While the growth percentage of air transportation stands at 5%, Emirates Airline is scoring 4 times this average.

513 | Emirates Airline is ranked 2nd among the most profitable world carriers and 20th in terms of size. During the 2005 fiscal year, it transported around 12.5 million passengers.

514 | **Emirates SkyCargo** has announced that it has met a record achievement of over $1 billion in revenue and 1 million tonnes of cargo with the announcement of this year's annual financial results for 2005-2006 fiscal year.

515 | "Meeting the milestone of $1 billion and 1 million tonnes is a direct reflection of our ability to meet the demands of our discerning customers, provide the necessary

Travel & Tourism

capacity for our growing network, and stand behind our reputation for delivery on a very high standard of service. Our achievement was made despite a host of challenges faced by the aviation industry last year, which makes us particularly proud."
Tim Clark, President, *Emirates Airline*

516 | Emirates SkyCargo's performance clearly indicated the dominance of the Asia-Pacific region, which contributed 41.6% of the revenue. Europe and the Americas contributed 19.3%, the Indian Sub-continent 14.6% and the Middle East & Africa 24.5%.

517 | Currently, Emirates SkyCargo freighters operate to 26 destinations. The carrier's fleet services 80 destinations in Europe, North America, Middle East, Africa, the Indian subcontinent and the Far East.

518 | Emirates Group has become the 1st Middle East air cargo and airline organization to achieve TAPA (Technology Asset Protection Association) certification, in recognition of high standards of security among its Dubai-based cargo operations.

DUBAI AIRPORT |

519 | By 2010, Dubai International Airport (DIA) will be handling 60 million passengers.

520 | A total of 24.7 million passengers used the Dubai International Airport in 2005, registering a 14% growth year-on-year, compared with 21.7 million passengers in 2004.

521 | The number of passengers in Dubai International Airport is expected to reach 29 million in 2006.

522 | Aircraft movement in Dubai was marked by an 11% growth, with 217,165 movements in 2005, compared to 195,820 movements in 2004.

523 | The $4.1 billion Dubai International Airport expansion program includes the construction of terminal 3, concourse 2 and concourse 3. The entire project is slated to be completed by 2007. Upon completion of the 2nd phase, Dubai International Airport will be able to handle 70 million passengers a year.

Travel & Tourism

524 | Currently, Dubai International Airport is the world's largest airport development project, with an average of 14,000 to 18,000 people working onsite.

525 | "Dubai International Airport is growing on average between 15% and 22% annually. And the airport's capacity is expected to increase to 70 million passengers annually." **Tim Clark,** President, *Emirates Airline*

526 | Dubai International Airport has become the 1st airport in the Middle East to join the Airport Services Quality (ASQ), a program that benchmarks airports on advanced technologies and processes. The program was launched by the Airport Council International, a global body representing airport authorities.

527 | There are 112 airline companies operating from Dubai to more than 165 destinations.

528 | "Dubai is among the few cities in the world to apply the open-skies policy. We are competing with more than 112 airline companies operating to and from Dubai, in a free and just environment, without receiving any special privileges." **Maurice Flanagan,** Executive Vice Chairman, *Emirates Airline & Group*

529 | Dubai Airport registered unprecedented growth rate in private aviation during 2005, reaching 57% (6,216 flights), compared to 3,940 flights during 2004. The number of flights is expected to reach 8,390 in 2006.

530 | Dubai International Airport has started to use the electronic gate (e-gate) system that operates on fingerprints and an e-card which carries the data of the residents. Experts believe that such a sophisticated electronic card system will help the government curb and monitor the activities of terrorist organizations or criminal suspects in a speedy and accurate way.

531 | The achievements of Dubai International Airport have been globally recognized with 44 major international awards since 1996. By 2005, DIA had won Business Traveler Germany, Best Airport Middle East, Best Airport Worldwide, Selling Long Haul-UK, Gold Award, Worldwide Airport, Buying Business Travel-UK and the World's Leading Airport & the Middle East's Leading Airport in the World Travel Awards as well as the Best Safety Initiative Award 2005.

532 | "While stronger Asian carriers such as Singapore Airlines and Cathay Pacific are still

growing, the Gulf upstarts are growing much faster. Over the past decade, traffic at Dubai has grown 500%, while Singapore's healthy growth is a bit over 50%."
Peter Harbison, Executive Chairman, *Center for Asia Pacific Aviation*

DUBAI CARGO VILLAGE |

533 | Located in Dubai International Airport, Dubai Cargo Village (DCV) registered 19.9% growth in 2005, handling 1.3 million tonnes of cargo, compared to the same period in 2004. It also registered record growth rates in delivery operations during 2005, reaching 12.5%.

534 | By the end of 2005, the new terminal's sewage, road works, foundations and other infrastructure developments were in line with the building set for completion in summer 2006 as part of the first phase of development. When completed, the Mega Terminal will put Dubai firmly in the top 6 cargo destinations in the world.

535 | "We expect to handle about 1.5 million tonnes of cargo in 2006. Right now 50% of the construction work at the Cargo Mega Terminal is completed. The big new facility will be ready to operate by next year increasing cargo handling capacity to 2.5 million tonnes per annum. For the record that volume of cargo throughput would eclipse airports such as LHR, JFK and even CDG."
Abdulla Mohammed Bin Khediya, Senior General Manager, *Dubai Cargo Village*

536 | In recent years, DCV has seen dramatic growth in the transportation of machinery, car spares as well as food, perishables and electronics. Today, Dubai Cargo village is ranked 18th in the world and has won 18 international awards to date.

DAFZA |

537 | Established in 1996, **Dubai Airport Free Zone Authority** (DAFZA) is a one-stop halt for online services, technological support, superb infrastructure, an excellent location within the boundaries of Dubai International Airport.

538 | DAFZA has recorded a 62% increase in the number of companies operating during 2005 compared to 2004. More than 318 multinational and regional companies have

been attracted to operate within the Free Zone boundaries during 2005, bringing the total number of companies operating in the Free Zone to 825.

539 | Some of DAFZA's major multinational companies include Airbus, Boeing, Audi, Applebee's, David Morris, DHL, Rolls-Royce and Parma International World.

540 | European companies operating in DAFZA represent about 34% of the total number of companies there, while Middle East and Gulf companies represent 32% and American companies 8%.

541 | "The aviation sector is rapidly growing throughout the entire region, therefore aviation and its related industries will be our main focus in the future. We already completed phases 4 and 5 of DAFZA and the 6th phase is to be completed mid 2006. We also have plans to build phases 7 and 8 towards 2007 to accommodate the large number of companies in the free zone."
Dr. Mohammed Al Zarouni, Director General, *DAFZA*

542 | Dubai's national airfreight handling company is one of the fastest growing companies in the region. Representing a large number of the world's leading airlines, **DNATA's** premises within DAFZA offer highly trained staff and dedicated equipment at its 9,000 sq. m Free Zone Logistics Center (FLC).

543 | Up till April 2006, the number of operators at **Freezone Logistics Center** was 48, the monthly flight frequency is more than 500, and annual cargo throughput exceeds 100,000 tonnes. When operational, the four-storey FLC III will extend existing FLC facilities to create a giant 47,000 sq. m warehouse and office complex and will more than triple annual throughput capacity of the FLC complex to a massive 500,000 tonnes.

544 | "Freezone Logistics Center (FLC) III, with its vastly enlarged capacity and sophisticated fully automated facilities, is fast becoming a reality and will transform cargo handling in Dubai. Airlines, agents, freight forwarders and charter operators will be able to complete their business transactions faster, with government agencies including customs, municipality, health and police located on the premises to provide round-the-clock services."
Jean Pierre L. de Pauw, Senior Vice President, *DNATA Cargo*

DUBAI WORLD CENTRAL |

545 | Dubai World Central, the $33 billion mega project, formerly known as Jebel Ali Airport City, is designed to support Dubai's aviation, tourism and logistics needs.

546 | Dubai World Central is more than just an airport. It's a new city unlike any other, it's a pioneering new transport hub that will transform the region into one of the most powerful global centers for logistics, tourism and commerce. Serving 120 million passengers and 12 million tonnes of cargo annually, it will be the world's 1st multi-modal logistics transport platform.

547 | Dubai World Central will include the following: Jebel Ali International Airport ($8.1 billion project), Logistics City, Enterprise Park, Residential City, Commercial City and a Golf Resort.

548 | Dubai World Central will include over 850 towers, a base for research and education, a center of finance, a residential city and a world-class golf resort. The city will become one of the most dynamic and vibrant work places in the world.

549 | Dubai World Central which is the size of London's Heathrow and Chicago's O'Hare airports combined, will operate as an independent free zone and will accommodate up to 750,000 residents and workers.

DUBAI AEROSPACE ENTERPRISE |

550 | Dubai stepped into a new phase of development with the announcement of Dubai Aerospace Enterprise (DAE), an investment vehicle to channel $15 billion aimed at creating a global aerospace manufacturing and services corporation, backed by the government of Dubai and the signatories to the agreement — Dubai International Capital, Emaar, Istithmar, Dubai International Financial Center (DIFC), Amlak Finance and the Dubai Airport Free Zone Authority (DAFZA).

551 | DAE, which plans to offer aviation services ranging from aircraft leasing to airport operations, expects to generate sales of up to $2 billion by 2016 by running airports in Asia. The consortium will invest up to $6 billion to develop airfields in Asia and is expected to earn $1.5 billion in sales from such operations.

552 | DAE is planning to buy 50 aircraft for lease to local and regional airlines and may purchase the fleet within 2 years.

553 | DAE is targeting the $100 billion global airport development and operations, aircraft leasing and financing, and specialist aerospace education and training segments.

554 | "The Dubai Aerospace Enterprise University (DAE University) is absolutely fundamental to the overall plan and will provide a stream of highly skilled, superbly trained and very able professionals from the region to support the developing industry. It is crucial that we are able to provide the means to enable homegrown talent to develop at home. Equally, we are proud to offer a facility that will contribute to the region's resources and add value to its human capital."
Dr. Mohammed Al Zarouni, Managing Director, *DAE and* Director General, *DAFZA*

TOURISM & HOTELS |

555 | "Dubai offers visitors a combination of things most cities don't have – safety; the old world charm of Arabia side by side with modernity; the best accommodation and entertainment facilities in the world; excellent infrastructure services for conducting business and a high standard of living."
Khalid A. Bin Sulayem, Director General, *DTCM*

556 | The Department of Tourism and Commerce Marketing (DTCM) figures prove that during 2005, Dubai's hotels recorded an average occupancy rate of 85%, leaving Dubai at the top of the world league for hotel occupancy, followed by New York with 83% and Singapore at 80%.

557 | For Dubai's 5-star hotels, the average occupancy level for December 2005 was 95% as against 89% recorded for the corresponding month in 2004.

558 | "The number of Dubai hotel guests reached 6.2 million in 2005, up from 5.4 million in 2004, an increase of 14%."
Khalid A. Bin Sulayem, Director General, *DTCM*

559 | The number of hotels in Dubai has risen from 276 with 26,155 rooms at the end of 2004 to 300 hotels with 29,834 rooms at the end of 2005.

560 | "Out of the 150 to 200 new hotels planned to open by 2010, 35 to 40 were confirmed to access the Dubai market by 2008. Moreover, the Emirate still needs to provide 80,000 more rooms to achieve its 15 million visitors target by 2010."
Gavin Samson, Associate Director, *TRI Hospitality Consulting*

561 | "I believe that the real estate coupled with the tourism boom in Dubai makes hotel apartments a very lucrative proposition. Hotel apartments are one of the fastest growing real estate sub-sectors in the world. According to Ministry of Planning forecasts, visitors in hotels and apartments in 2004 stood at 5.5 million and are expected to touch 8.5 million by 2010."
Abuali Shroff, Managing Director, *Sheffield Real Estate*

562 | Dubai is expected to see an estimated 18,000 to 20,000 more hotel rooms by 2010, an increase of almost 100%, fueling the risk of oversupply, according to a report prepared by international consultants, HVS International in early 2006.

563 | "In all, over 25,000 rooms and suites will be added to the existing regional hotel room stock by 2008. From boutique to chic, and from colossal to mind-blowing, the rate and variety of development is astounding. This is before we add Dubailand to the equation. This project alone will add another 50 hotels by 2010."
Bernard Walsh, Managing Director, *DMG world media Dubai*

564 | For Dubai, Germany is the 2nd largest source market in Europe. In the 1st half of 2005, there was a 24% increase in the number of German guests staying in Dubai hotels, and a 55% increase was recorded in the number of tour operators promoting Dubai in Germany.

565 | Europe is considered the main feeder for the 5-star hotel market in Dubai, accounting for 47% of total demand. The GCC and non-GCC Arab countries, account for another 27%. Published plans also seek to attract the Turkish, Pakistani, Indian, Chinese and Iranian markets over the next 3 to 5 years. The government is also working on developing the cruise market in Dubai.

566 | A 2-day tourism visit to Dubai costs an average of $410 (AED 1,505) in a 5-star hotel with 14 different offers and services. The global average for a similar visit is about $470.

567 | "The tourism and hotel sectors directly contribute by 19% to Dubai's GDP, while their indirect contribution stands at 32% from the GDP."
Khalid Bin Sulayem, Director General, *DTCM*

568 | Dubai has one 7-star hotel, 35 5-star hotels, 31 4 star hotels, 42 3-star hotels, 44 2-star hotels and 83 1-star hotels. It is worth noting that the number of 5-star hotels is likely to double in the next few years.

569 | Jumeirah Properties, the Dubai based luxury international hospitality group encompasses the world renowned Burj Al Arab, the world's most luxurious hotel, the multi-award winning Jumeirah Beach Hotel, Jumeirah Emirates Towers, Jumeirah Beach Club Resort and Spa, Madinat Jumeirah and Jumeirah Bab Al Shams Desert Resort & Spa, in addition to Wild Wadi, regarded as one of the premier water parks outside of North America.

570 | Jumeirah Emirates Towers, one of Dubai's major landmarks, was voted Best Business Hotel in the Middle East and Best Business Hotel in Dubai for the year 2006 by readers of Business Traveller Magazine Asia and Business Traveller Magazine UK.

571 | Among the new hotels due to be inaugurated in the next 3 years, are the 335-room **Armani Hotel** which will open at Burj Dubai in 2008, the **Versace Hotel** which will open in 2008 with 220 rooms and 204 villas, and the 350-room Conrad Hotel run by Hilton International and due to open in 2007.

572 | **Rotana** Hotels and Resorts, the region's largest home-grown hotel management chain, will roll out a new budget hotel chain, Centro, involving 25 hotels to be built at a cost of AED 2.2 billion ($594 million) in the UAE in the next 5 years. Currently, Rotana Hotels and Resorts operate 22 hotels in and outside of the UAE and 21 are under construction. By the end of 2008, the number of hotels will increase to 43.

573 | **IFA Hotels & Resorts** announced that it is investing AED 1.6 billion ($450 million) to establish Fairmont Palm Hotel and Resort. The project will be completed in early 2008. It includes 400 luxurious hotel rooms, in addition to the Fairmont Palm Residence, comprising 558 apartments, a townhouse and a penthouse.

574 | Operating more than 850 luxury hotels around the world, **Starwood Hotels & Resorts,** is shifting its regional office from Cairo to Dubai as part of a major restructuring of its operations in the Middle East where the group is poised to double its portfolio to 100 properties in 5 years.

575 | **Mövenpick,** with 10 new hotels in the Gulf Co-operation Council (GCC), of which no less than 7 are in Dubai, is a true vote of confidence for the Gulf's largest and most happening urban hotel market.

576 | Dubai's hotels and hotel apartments have been ranked the world's 1st in terms of generating the highest RevPar between January and September 2005. Each room generates $175.47. Dubai comes ahead of New York and Paris, where a hotel room in each of these cities generates $163.32 and $169.53 respectively.

577 | Dubai and the UAE as a whole are the most popular destinations for all nationalities, especially when considering hotel timeshare purchase. With regard to fractional ownership, one of the most attractive locations is Dubai.

578 | Restaurant and fast food business in Dubai recorded an annual growth of 27% in 2005 and this is attributed to the growing population and the booming tourism sector which is creating new opportunities for several international restaurant chain owners to open their outlets in the UAE.

MARITIME TOURISM |

579 | The UAE marine travel business alone is worth some $11 billion per annum.

580 | "I expect maritime tourism in Dubai to witness momentous growth next year, as the annual number of ships anchoring in the Emirate sees a hike from 6 to 17, and the number of passengers increases to between 12,000 and 13,000."
Awadh Al Ketbi, Acting Manager, *Cruise Terminal*

581 | An estimated 25,000 new berths for boats will be built over the next 5 years in the UAE. In Dubai alone, mega-projects such as the **Dubai Marina**, The Palms and the Dubai Festival City will feature large marinas, capable of hosting thousands of boats.

582 | At present, Dubai urgently needs 10,000 new docks.

583 | "When all the Palm projects on the maritime façade are completed, it is expected that there will be more than 40,000 berths to meet the demand of entertainment boats."
Ali Said Bin Thalith, General Manager, *Nakheel Marinas*

584 | "We have conducted a very detailed feasibility study about prospects for the yacht industry in Dubai and some of the other key Gulf markets. Everything points to an explosion of demand for yachts and the specialized services that go along with marine-themed developments such as The Palm Jumeirah, The Palm Jebel Ali, The Palm Deira and the World islands from Nakheel, as well as developments from Emaar properties."
Imtiaz Panjwani, Managing Director, *Pegasus Holdings*

585 | "Dubai will have a major leisure boating industry within 5-10 years."
Joe Goddard, General Manager, Dubai Marina Yacht Club

586 | The emergence of Dubai as an international tourism destination, the powerful marketing behind the Emirate, strong investment and a maturing of interest in boating and marina lifestyles would be key driving factors in the leisure boating industry of the future.

587 | In 2005, Dubai Marina was expected to include around 250 berths, Dubai International Marine Club with 200 berths, Jebel Ali Marina with 150 berths, Dubai Offshore Sailing Club with 80 berths (for its exclusive members) and Jumeirah Beach Hotel with 60 berths, all currently mobilized and almost full to capacity. Additionally, as the Palm Islands, The World and Palm Island 2 take shape there will be a full fledged berthing place. In five years, more than 3,000 berths are expected to be completed.

588 | Upon completion of its projects in the next 5 years, Dubai Marina will be one of the world's largest waterfront developments.

DUBAILAND |

589 | A destination of extraordinary vision, Dubailand is the largest and most innovative leisure and entertainment tourist attraction in the region. Divided into 5 theme worlds, and comprising more than 26 mega projects, Dubailand will feature state-of-the-art sporting facilities, and world-first concepts, including giant theme parks, eco-tourism resorts, shopping and recreation venues. Dubailand will be inaugurated in 2008.

590 | Dubailand, spread over 3 billion sq. ft (280 sq. km), is more than 68,870 acres, more than 107 sq. m, bigger than 52,000 football fields, bigger than two San Franciscos, bigger

than four and a half Manhattans, 100 times the size of Monaco, bigger than Disneyland and Disney World combined.

591 │ "Dubailand will be one of the top 5 destinations in the world for family entertainment, tourism and leisure."
Salem Bin Dasmal, Chief Executive Officer, *Dubailand*

592 │ Dubailand is a massive, sprawling, and totally built-from-scratch city-as-tourist attraction that suggests the theme-park atmosphere of Disney World or Las Vegas, only more so.

593 │ Dubailand will host **Aqua Dunya**, a $1.9 billion gigantic water theme park resort of 8 million sq. ft that will be the largest in the Middle East. To be completed by 2008, the project expects to welcome 1.3 million theme park visitors in its 1st year and 3 million annually in coming years.

594 │ The **"City of Arabia"** project, covering an area of 20 million sq. ft in Dubailand, is due to attract some AED 7.2 billion ($2 billion) in investments. The project will include one of the world's largest shopping centers, as well as an international dinosaur entertainment city, which has been designed in cooperation with the London National History Museum. Once completed, the project will provide housing to more than 35,000 people.

595 │ **Falcon City of Wonders**, the 41 million sq. ft project in Dubailand, will feature cultural facilities with structures based on famous sites and the architectural marvels of the world, such as the Pyramids, the Eiffel Tower, the Hanging Gardens of Babylon, the Taj Mahal and the Leaning Tower of Pisa.

596 │ "Falcon City of Wonders, the AED 5.5 billion ($1.5 billion) community project being built in Dubailand, will be at the forefront of this growth in the city's tourism sector. It is the only project to feature life-size replicas of the wonders of the world, rendering it a truly unique attraction."
Salem Al Moosa, Chairman and CEO, *Falcon City of Wonders*

597 │ Investments in the 24.71 million sq. ft **Legends** project in Dubailand are expected to reach about AED 14 billion ($3.8 billion), including 3 main theme parks, leisure village, a golf course and the Legends residences and businesses.

598 | **Al Barari**, the 14.2 million sq. ft project, with $654 million in investments, includes a lush habitat of plants, desert vegetation and an eco-tourism project, to be built in Dubailand. Its key features include 16 different varieties of gardens from all across the world, a cultural amphitheater, integrative medicine, a health spa and a life style retail center.

599 | **Islamic Culture & Science World** spread over 1.93 million sq. ft in Dubailand, provides state-of-the-art facilities for the promotion, understanding and research of Space, Natural and Human Sciences, as well as Islamic Culture, Arts and Literature. It includes a multi-purpose stage, International Cultural & Scientific Center, exhibition area, museum, labs and other relevant facilities.

600 | **Beautyland,** a 3.48 million sq. ft project, is an exclusive and luxury complex in Dubailand containing an international array of branded beauty-themed spas providing relaxation treatments, and holistic therapies along with health and organic nutrition. The project will also feature: a Beauty Museum, a Beauty Academy, a Boutique Hotel and a boulevard where an exclusive selection of cosmetic and luxury brands will be sold.

601 | The 4.14 million sq. ft Dubailand project, **Dubai Lifestyle City**, will house the 1st, one-of -its-kind World Class IMG Sports Academy in the region. It will be home to an exclusive boutique 7-star hotel with a destination spa and a premium retail walkway offering exclusive sports and wellness products and services.

SPORTS |

602 | **Dubai Sports City** (DSC) is the region's premier sporting venue featuring 4 giant-sized stadiums designed for international events including soccer, hockey, cricket and rugby.

603 | Dubai Sports City the cornerstone project of Dubailand, will feature a series of major sports academy facilities including: the 1st project-built Manchester United Soccer School anywhere in the world; a David Lloyd Tennis Academy; a Butch Harmon School of Golf, the first such facility outside the United States; the International Cricket Council's own ICC global cricket academy; top class multi-sport training facilities including gymnasium and a swimming pool; and a world-class sports rehabilitation center.

604 | "Dubai Sports City, costing $2.5 billion and sprawling over 50 million sq. ft, aspires to be a bustling mini-metropolis devoted to sports, a Xanadu for spectators and participants when it partly opens next year."
The New York Times

605 | Dubai Golf City, part of "Dubailand" extends over a 55 million sq. ft area and costs around AED 6.5 billion ($1.77 billion).

606 | "The entrepreneurial spirit that built America lives on in Dubai. Sport is a multi-trillion-dollar business, and Dubai can profitably serve as the nexus between the Northern and Southern hemispheres."
U. Balasubramaniam, Chief Executive Officer, *Dubai Sports City*

607 | Dubai Snowdome, the AED 3.7 billion ($1 billion) gigantic indoor ski dome project, covers an area of 1.36 million sq. ft (126,347 sq. m) and consists of the largest free-standing see-through dome structure in the world with more than 200 m diameter and 70 m height. The ski dome will feature only real snow, around 6,000 tonnes (5.5 million kg), in its +10 degrees Centigrade winter environment.

608 | The Snowdome will include a rotating sky deck, mountain run, training area, snow play area, toboggan run, penguinarium, ice skating rink, ice skating adventure area and a flying theater featuring a virtual flight over the Atlantic. It will be surrounded by 9 Iceberg Residence towers and will be flanked by 2 Crystal Towers, all with winter themed architecture.

609 | Everyone who plays at the Dubai Tennis Championships have nothing but praise for the tournament which continues to go from strength to strength, attracting the biggest names in tennis to the UAE. Jennifer Capriatti said her experience of Dubai was like being in an Aladdin movie, and Martina Navratilova was pleasantly surprised at the melting pot of cultures. Fabrice Santoro said he could live in Dubai, and Tim Henman said he felt safer than he does in London.

610 | A new body established to oversee Dubai's vibrant golfing industry made its international debut at the 2005 Open Championship at St. Andrews. The new organization – to be known as **'Golf in DUBAI'** (GiD) – has been created to act as the international representative of all Dubai's golf clubs, while at the same time promoting Dubai as a unique golfing destination.

Travel & Tourism

611 | Dubailand concluded an agreement with **Great Wheel Corporation** for the establishment of the world's biggest Ferris Wheel, which is due to open in 2008.

612 | When fully completed in 2018, Dubailand will employ an estimated 300,000 people, cater to 200,000 visitors a day and attract 15 million people a year from 2010 spending on average $100 each.

DSF / DSS |

613 | Over 2,300 retail outlets participate in the **Dubai Shopping Festival** (DSF), offering goods and services ranging from gold, jewelry, electronics, cars, cosmetics, textiles, and handicrafts, at big cash discounts. Travel and tourism companies also offer discounted flights and excursions for those wishing to visit Dubai during the festival. Around 300 hotels in Dubai also participate in the festival by offering deals for hotel accommodation.

614 | "Dubai Shopping Festival is a perfect example of the Dubai Brand. Universal brotherhood, happiness, excitement, joy and adventure are the signature trademarks of DSF. The festival itself became a tribute to the inherent passion, ambition and strength of the people of the UAE."
Laila Suhail, Chief Marketing Officer, *Dubai Shopping Festival*

615 | The **Dubai Summer Surprises** (DSS) and DSF are among the brand ambassadors of Dubai reassuring its position as the tourism hub of the region. DSS today has redefined the summer season in Dubai as a vibrant and happening time with a whole lot of activities to keep both children and adults creatively occupied. DSF too has reinvented itself over the years and graduated from being a retail event to a retail-cum-entertainment extravaganza. The steady progression of the two events goes to show their success over the past several years.

616 | "Dubai buzzes with activity throughout the year. During summer too, Dubai hotels have shown very high occupancy rates, clearly reflecting the popularity of the Emirate. DSS is largely responsible for attracting tourists during the peak summer season. Worth noting is the turnout of visitors from the GCC especially families who come to Dubai during the DSS to partake in the fun, entertainment and shopping opportunities. DSS today is an event with mass appeal."
Mohammed Khamis Bin Hareb, Executive Director of Operations and Marketing, *DTCM*

617 | "Over the years, Dubai Summer Surprises (DSS) has become an event to reckon with, getting bigger with each passing year. And the figures this time are expected to be over 10% in terms of the total spend and visitor turnover. The number of visitors to DSS 2005 was 1.5 million and the total spend was a whopping AED 1.72 billion."
Laila Suhail, Executive Director of Project, *Dubai Summer Surprises*

DUBAI FESTIVAL CITY |

618 | A 1,600 acre city-within-a-city, Dubai Festival City is an inspirational all-in-one destination taking shape on the sweeping curves of the historic Dubai Creek with total investments of around $10 billion.

619 | "Banks will finance nearly 60% of the $10 billion needed to develop Dubai Festival City, which is under development. The rest, 40%, would be financed by Al Futtaim Group, the developer of the project."
Marwan Shehadeh, Managing Director, *Al Futtaim Capital*

620 | In Dubai Festival City, some 20,000 homes of diverse design will be leased forming an integral part of a city where, when completed, over 77,000 people will live, work, shop, dine and relax.

621 | Dubai Festival City will be home to the largest hospitality cluster in the Middle East consisting of over 2,500 rooms managed by some of the world's leading hotel operators such as Four Seasons Hotels & Resorts, the first for the luxury brand in the UAE, Crowne Plaza, InterContinental and W Hotels.

622 | Dubai Festival City unveiled, in September 2005, an AED 6 billion ($1.6 billion) "Marsa Al Khor" neighbourhood – a 245,000 sq.m, upmarket, contemporary waterfront community reminiscent of some of the world's finest lifestyle destinations, including Cape Town's Waterfront and Sydney Harbour. Furthermore, it announced an AED 1.4 billion "Hillside Community" residential project – a stunning, 36 hectare village of Gulf Arabian-style homes on a man-made hill in the heart of the development.

623 | The vibrant centerpiece in Dubai Festival City, the Festival Center, will feature over 450 shops and services and more than 90 restaurants and cafés boasting some of the world's best brands.

624 | The Festival Center in Dubai Festival City will be linked to the iconic convention hotel, Intercontinental Dubai Festival City, being built at a cost of more than AED 600 million ($163.5 million) on the north-west peninsula of the 150-berth Mediterranean Festival Marina. The hotel, which will open in January 2007, will have 424 rooms, a 4,500 sq. m convention center and will include 90 serviced apartments.

GLOBAL VILLAGE |

625 | Global Village is a huge cultural entertainment center spread over 16.7 million sq. ft that consists of huge pavilions representing 160 countries around the world. It brings together diverse merchandise and cultures covering a broad spectrum of activities including music, dances, arts and handicrafts, theater, costumes and cuisine of different countries.

626 | In 2005, the Global Village celebrated its 10th anniversary and welcomed 5 million visitors, and in 2004, this crowd-drawing mega event generated around $90 million in 23 days.

627 | It's probably the only place in the world where you can buy an intricately woven Indian pashmina shawl, a Japanese bonsai, fresh Canadian Maple Syrup, spices from Iran and olive oil from Palestine, all from the same place.

CULTURE VILLAGE |

628 | Dubai Properties launched an AED 50 billion ($13.6 billion) Culture Village, a unique development offering an elite lifestyle in an intellectually stimulating environment, with year-round world class cultural events. It will be located along the Dubai Creek next to Garhoud Bridge on an area of 40 million sq. ft.

629 | "Culture Village will be a tourist landmark that will attract culture and art lovers from all over the world. HH Sheikh Mohammed initiated the development of Culture Village because of the important role that culture and arts play in developing nations. The project will add diversity to the cultural and art scene in the UAE and the region."
Hashim Al Dabbal, CEO, *Dubai Properties*

Travel & Tourism

MEDIA & IT | 7

Media & IT

Dubai, Connecting People...The UAE was ranked number one in technology in the 2005 Arab Competitiveness Report. Etisalat has pumped in more than $5 billion into the telecom network and now the country's mobile penetration rate is nearly 100%. The UAE IT services market grew by 10% to $2.7 billion in 2005. Dubai Media City (DMC) houses more than 1,000 companies comprising publishing houses, TV stations, broadcasting corporations, media, advertising & marketing companies where around 400 publications are produced.

"Here in Dubai, we have access to some of the best and brightest minds in the region, and from around the world. The time is right for us to tap into this creativity, and take up the challenge of growth to create a city that is truly unique in the world — not just a city made of glass, steel and concrete, but a city made of ideas, creativity and opportunity."

HH Sheikh Ahmed Bin Saeed Al Maktoum, President, *Department of Civil Aviation* and Chairman and CEO, *Emirates Group*

OVERVIEW |

630 | "There are cities in the world, and there are cities of the world. Dubai is synonymous with growth, communications and, definitely, advertising. Nobody offers the advertising industry as much as Dubai."
Joseph Ghossoub, Chairman and World President, IAA

631 | "It will be the best because Sheikh Mohammed wills it. It will keep growing bigger and better. I am amazed by what is happening here in Dubai, amazed at the ideas and the plans to sustain those ideas. It is a place of interesting extremes."
Morgan Freeman, Hollywood Actor and Producer

632 | According to a study by Rutgers University, New Jersey, Dubai's key information and communication technology (ICT) indicators, particularly its mobile phone density and internet penetration, are comparable to those of key cities in the most developed countries. Dubai's mobile penetration rate is higher than the average mobile penetration rate in Western Europe which varies between 80% and 82%.

633 | While the free zones in Dubai are expected to create 150,000 new jobs during the next 3 years, Dubai International Financial Center, Dubai Internet City and Dubai Media City together are expected to create additional 135,000 new jobs.

634 | "The media explosion will shift communication and Dubai stands as the face of the future. I was here in Dubai 6 years ago. I see energy, strength, power and optimism, whereas in Europe we will not see such changes for the next 50 years or so."
Maurice Levy, Chief Executive Officer, *Publicis Groupe*

Media & IT

E-GOVERNMENT |

635 | The UAE has been named as one of the world's top countries in terms of e-government readiness in a recent report published by the United Nations Online Public Network and Finance (UNPAN) agency. The UAE, which gained 2.17 points topping the Arab countries and ranking 21st internationally, precedes Japan which gained 2.12 points and Russia which gained 1.89 points.

636 | Dubai e-Government has succeeded in launching several novel knowledge-oriented projects that have left their traces in the community, such as "the e-Citizen", "the e-Employee", "the e-Library" and "e-4All". All these projects have contributed to the eradication of electronic illiteracy in the community.

637 | Dubai e-Government's strategic goal is to provide 90% of Government services through electronic channels, including Web, mobile devices and fixed line telephones, by the end of 2007.

638 | "The success achieved by Dubai e-Government in recent years in promoting the adoption of e-Services among Dubai's residents, has been commendable, especially at a time when Dubai is progressing towards the formation of a digital society."
Salem Al Shair, Director, e-Services, *Dubai e-Government (named 'Young CEO of the Year' at the Third Middle East CEO of the Year Awards)*

639 | "Dubai e-Government will continue to enhance the e-Services experience through improved synergistic tools and shared best practices among government departments. These tools include e-Integrate, an electronic business integration service to enable workflow-based electronic documents processing; e-Delivery, an electronic processing system for courier services, e-Jawaz, an electronic authentication, single sign-on and authorization service and e-Feedback, an electronic service to gauge satisfaction levels to e-Services."
Mahmood Al Bastaki, Acting Director of e-Services, *Dubai e-Government*

640 | E-illiteracy no longer exists in Dubai, since the e-transformation process has led to transparency and social interaction. In light of Dubai's e-Government, the principle of customer satisfaction and high quality has become widespread and Dubai has become a symbol of the knowledge renaissance.

641 | "We cannot claim to have achieved 100% of the target (70% of e-Government services

by 2005) so far. In fact, we can say that at this moment (August 2005) not less than 55% of government services are available through non-traditional channels."
Salem Al Shair, Director of e-Services, *Dubai e-Government*

642 | Today, **Dubai Municipality** provides more than 381 online services as part of the e-Government initiative and this includes 238 transactional services, 50 interactive services and 93 informational services in the fields of engineering, environment, planning, public health and finance.

643 | Up till March 2006, more than 16,779 registered business users from 6,461 companies and nearly 5,000 public users benefited from e-Municipality services.

644 | "Our aim is to have maximum online clients so that we can improve customer service, improve our processes, and reduce costs by saving time, money and efforts. Now, as we are in Phase 4 of the e-Government initiative, we are having a total revamp of the e-government IT infrastructure and are reviewing our e-government strategy through 2007."
Hussein Nasser Lootah, Acting Director General, *Dubai Municipality*

645 | DCCI has declared that most of their services will soon go online including the Membership Registration, Attestations and Country of Origin Certificates Issuance for the purpose of facilitating the procedures for DCCI members and clients.

646 | Dubai was ranked 18th among the top 20 cities in terms of digital governance, making it 1st among its Arab peers, by Rutgers University (State University of New Jersey).

TELECOM |

647 | The number of mobile phone subscribers in the UAE increased by more than 23% reaching more than 4.5 million by the end of 2005. Until February 2006, the penetration rate was 98%.

648 | The UAE benefits from a high tele-density and the sector as a whole has shown a 12% year-on-year growth in value.

649 | Established in 1976, Emirates Telecommunications Co. (Etisalat) operates, maintains and develops the national and international fixed-line network, mobile telephony and

internet access in the UAE. Etisalat reported a 31% profit surge to AED 1.337 billion ($364 million) for the 1st quarter 2006.

650 | Etisalat has earned total revenue of AED 12.9 billion ($3.5 billion) and gross profits of AED 8.5 billion ($2.3 billion) in 2005, before payment of 50% of gross profit as royalty to the UAE federal government. The 2005 figures indicate an increase in total revenue and gross profits of 23% and 25% respectively. Earnings per share also increased from AED 0.94 in 2004 to AED 1.17 in 2005.

651 | Etisalat, which is 60% owned by the federal government and has a total capital of AED 4 billion, has pumped in more than $5 billion over the past decade to make the UAE's telecommunications sector, including mobile phone services, boom.

652 | "We know that a 2nd operator will eventually enter the UAE market. That's why we have continuously improved our efficiencies to maintain our customer base and give handsome pay-outs to our shareholders."
Mohammed Hassan Omran, Chairman and CEO, *Etisalat*

653 | The Middle East Excellence Awards Institute has announced that Etisalat is a winner of the GCC Economic Award 2006.

654 | "Etisalat has set an example for many other corporations and companies in the region. It plays a key role in improving the telecom sector through high-quality technologies and customer services."
Ali Mohammed Al Kamali, Director, *Middle East Excellence Awards Institute*

655 | In April 2004, a presidential decree cancelled Etisalat's monopoly and in October 2004 the Telecom Regulatory Authority (TRA) was set up to oversee the introduction of competition and manage the frequency spectrum in the country.

656 | The UAE's 2nd telecommunications operator, Emirates Integrated Telecommunication Company (EITC), operating under the brand name **"du"**, is expected to start commercial operations by the middle of 2006. EITC will have a paid-up capital of AED 4 billion ($1.1 billion).

657 | "du", the Emirates Integrated Telecommunications Company (EITC) initial public offering was 167 times oversubscribed, with total applications amounting to more than $108 billion. The IPO was the largest ever in the UAE, according to investment banker EFG-Hermes. More than 225,000 investors applied for shares.

658 | "Competition is already there but we will not break the market rules to attract customers. We will not begin a price war with Etisalat. We bought TeCom Investments Company for AED 1.2 billion. We also have nearly 20,000 customers."
Ahmad Bin Bayat, Chairman, *Emirates Integrated Telecommunication Company (EITC)*

659 | According to a feasibility study "du" is expected to earn nearly AED 2.99 billion by the end of the 3rd year, when it will become profitable.

660 | Fixed line services in 2005 also saw a marginal growth of 4% to reach 1.2 million installed lines. Total internet connections, including high-speed internet access, crossed the 500,000 mark during the year.

661 | The MotoWithMe report, released by Motorola, reveals that Dubai and the UAE is one of the most highly mobile and connected societies in Europe, Middle East and Africa (EMEA) region.

662 | General Packet Radio Service (GPRS) users in Dubai and the UAE are estimated to be 200,000, according to a report by Madar Research Group in 2005.

TECHNOLOGY |

663 | The Networked Readiness Index (NRI) used in the Global Information Technology Report 2005-2006, one of the World Economic Forum's annual reports, and a valuable and unique benchmarking tool to determine national ICT strengths and weaknesses and to evaluate progress, ranks the UAE in the 28th position with a score of 0.54.

664 | Spending on IT services in Dubai and the UAE has amounted to approximately AED 7.35 billion ($2 billion), representing 34% of the Gulf total spending. Furthermore, the IT services market in the UAE grew by 10% in 2005 and is expected to have reached $2.7 billion by the end of that year.

665 | The UAE was ranked 1st in technology, according to the Arab World Competitiveness Report 2005 published by the World Economic Forum.

666 | With the total PC market increasing at a rate of 20% annually in the Middle East, Fujitsu Siemens Computers plans to open a computer factory in Dubai that will produce about 100,000 units per year.

667 | "The **Dubai Police Center** is among 170 such centers set up by Siemens around the world, including high-tech centers in Finland, Singapore, China, Norway and Germany and the complete integrated security systems for the 2004 Olympic Games in Athens, Greece."
Peter Fuchs, Chief Executive Officer, *Siemens*

668 | "Although the key IT markets of Saudi Arabia and the UAE are increasingly saturated, they will stay dynamic by adopting new technologies, undertaking upgrades, and through server message block (SMB) purchasing of the hardware necessary for staying competitive in the increasingly technology-dependent economy".
Roshana Rehan, Research Analyst, *IDC's Systems Group*

669 | The UAE's Telecommunications Regulatory Authority (TRA) has acquired the rights to 225 terrestrial TV channels out of the 236 present in the UHF and VHF bands. The UAE is expected to switch to a digital terrestrial broadcasting system within 2 years as part of an overall strategy to enhance the telecommunications sector in the country.

DUBAI SILICON OASIS |

670 | Dubai Silicon Oasis (DSO) is commited to creating the world's most integrated microelectronics technology park to provide end-to-end shared turnkey facilities for the semi-conductor industry.

671 | "Dubai Silicon Oasis is a creative society driven by the new and advanced technologies, covering a total area of 7.2 million sq. m. Thus, the Oasis investments are projected to exceed $10 billion during the next 20 years."
Issa Bastaki, Technology and Development Managing Director, *DSO*

672 | "We are spending AED 1.2 billion in infrastructure, the head office and the construction of 560 villas at DSO. If everything works out as planned, we would attract between $2 to $4 billion in total investment at the DSO. We have already signed up 80 companies which will rise to 100 in the coming months and bring in between 1,000 to 1,500 qualified professionals, designers and engineers. We are trying to tap the $250 billion semi-conductor and $8 billion global silicon manufacturing market."
Jurgen Knorr, Chief Executive Officer, *Dubai Silicon Oasis Authority (DSOA)*

Media & IT

673 | "DSO has, and is developing, all the necessary ingredients to build a next-generation global electronics hub. The team has done its homework and will be offering the world's most economic infrastructure for electronic innovation."
Jack Harding, Chief Executive Officer, *Silicon Valley-based e-Silicon*

674 | Dubai Silicon Oasis (DSO) established the Microelectronics Training Academy (MTA), a specialized educational initiative with the mission to promote, encourage, facilitate and inspire the development and creation of a skilled microelectronics workforce in the UAE and the region.

675 | DVD and CD manufacturer Planet Optical Disc is planning to create a 2nd facility with an AED 1 billion investment at the Dubai Silicon Oasis (DSO), which will be one of the largest of its kind in the region.

INTERNET |

676 | "Today internet usage penetration in the UAE stands at 47.2%. Our major focus in this area is to increase penetration levels by making broadband more attractive and affordable to our customers so that they can benefit from always-on, secure and high-speed internet connectivity."
Ahmad Abdulkarim Julfar, General Manager, *e-Company*

677 | In line with Dubai's liberal economic regime and regulations, **Dubai Internet City,** offers foreign companies 100% tax-free ownership, 100% repatriation on capital and profits, no currency restrictions, easy registration and licensing, stringent cyber regulations, protection of intellectual property, and most importantly, access to an ever-growing market of over 1.8 billion people.

678 | Launched in the year 2000, Dubai Internet City (DIC) provides a strategic and cost effective platform for ICT companies targeting emerging markets in a vast region extending from the Middle East to the Indian subcontinent, and from Africa to Central Asia. The cluster comprises companies from a variety of sectors - Software Development, Business Services, Web Based and e-Commerce, Consultancy, Sales and Marketing and Back Office.

679 | "Intel is moving its offices to Dubai Internet City because it offers a strategic platform to tap new opportunities in this fast-growing market."
Gordon Graylish, Vice President of the Sales and Marketing Group, and General Manager for EMEA, *Intel*

680 | Within a short span of time, a dynamic international community of Information Communication and Technology (ICT) companies has established itself in Dubai Internet City. The global ICT giants are all there: Microsoft, Oracle, HP, IBM, Compaq, Dell, Siemens, Canon, Logica, Sony Ericsson and Cisco Systems, to name just a few. These companies represent a formidable community of over 14,000 knowledge workers.

KNOWLEDGE VILLAGE |

681 | Dubai Knowledge Village (KV) was set up to develop Dubai into a destination for education for both regional and international learners. This new education and training hub is also set up to complement the free zone's other 2 clusters: Dubai Internet City and Dubai Media City by providing the facilities to train the clusters' future knowledge workers.

682 | Dubai Knowledge Village is home to regional branches of 15 prominent international universities from Australia, India, Pakistan, Iran, Russia, Belgium, UK, Ireland and Canada, offering advanced programs in fields such as Computing, Technology, Business Management, Life Science, Fashion, Media and many others.

683 | As a leading center for knowledge, Dubai Knowledge Village has also attracted around 109 professional training institutes and 54 human resource training centers and 89 learning support entities.

684 | From all corners of the world, students are traveling to Dubai Knowledge Village to study, coming from places such as Middle East, North Africa, the Asian Subcontinent, Iran, CIS, China, Europe and Australia.

685 | "In the Middle East, there is growing interest in high-quality European education. We are keen to establish partnerships with leading universities that can provide educational choices here in the region on par with what they provide in their home countries. Our emphasis is on creating a pool of educational offerings that is nothing short of the best available anywhere in the world."
Dr. Abdulla Al Karam, Chief Executive Officer, *Dubai Knowledge Village*

MEDIA |

686 | As a dedicated media zone, DMC ensures that all media businesses are given the "Freedom to Create".

687 | **Dubai Media City** (DMC) offers a one-stop-shop for setting up businesses without the bureaucracy, leaving partners to do what they do best: create. The hassle-free completion of formalities can be done in no time at all, without the need to visit individual government departments.

688 | The number of partners in Dubai Media City grew 20%, from 880 in 2004 to approximately 1,077 in 2005. In total, 75% of available space is set aside for new companies and the remaining 25% is reserved for companies already operating.

689 | In Dubai Media City there are around 450 publications, 140 TV stations, 55 broadcasting corporations, 343 media, advertisements and marketing companies.

690 | **Dubai Studio City** is an independent Broadcast Boutique. Designed to accelerate the growth of the broadcast, film, television and music production industries, it will be an ultra-modern facility integrating every component under one roof. Spread across 22 million sq. ft, it will also have residential areas, hotels, an entertainment center, film schools and training institutes.

691 | "Not only are direct opportunities in the music, film and broadcast sectors expected to increase, as the project starts developing there will also be a need for administrative and logistical skills and resources. The accelerated growth of the film, broadcast and music production industries will give rise to the need for more talent."
Dr. Amina Al Rustamani, Executive Director, *Dubai Studio City*

692 | Dubai's **International Media Production Zone** (IMPZ) seeks to create a unique cluster environment for media production companies from across the industry value chain, and from across the world, to interact and collaborate effectively. Catering exclusively to companies in the 3P industries – Printing, Publishing and Packaging – IMPZ is an initiative of the visionary Dubai government, under the patronage of the parent company, Dubai Holding.

693 | The International Media Production Zone (IMPZ) will float tenders for a number of projects in coming years as part of its AED 5 billion ($1.36 billion) development. IMPZ's own investment in infrastructure is going to touch $273 million over the next 2 years, including the $82 million contract awarded to Wade Adams Contracting.

694 | Reflecting the strong investor sentiment that the project is generating across the region, IMPZ announced key deals with leading global players, including Thomson Group, Al Ghurair Printing, Heidelberg, Galadari Investment, DynaGraph and Express Printing, for the development's printing, packaging and publishing clusters. Giffin Graphics, Emirates Printing Press, MANRolland, Agfa Pre-Press, Fuji, Kodak-Creo and Vimpex.

695 | "There are at least 340 printing houses here and it is a highly competitive market. Even Germany is not moving this fast."
Hamad Al Huraiz, Executive Director, *International Media Production Zone (IMPZ)*

696 | Dubai's Printing Industry has grown by an impressive 40% in the past 2 years, to constitute an estimated $133.5 million market, calculated on the basis of raw material imports.

697 | The printing and publishing industry has a huge potential for business in the Middle East region. Dubai is targeting about 300 million people in the Middle East and nearly 2 billion people in the Indian Subcontinent and Iran. In the last couple of years, the publishing industry has registered a growth rate of about 42% in the UAE alone.

698 | "UAE's printing and flexible packaging market is growing at 25% year on year and is worth AED 8 billion annually. Dubai represents about 70% of the country's printing and packaging businesses."
Ahmad Hassan Bin Al Sheikh, Chairman, *Printers Association*

ADVERTISEMENT |

699 | "You have to accept that Dubai has become the ad capital of the Middle East. It used to be Lebanon, now it is Dubai."
Joseph Ghossoub, Chairman and World President, IAA

700 | The total advertisement spending in the UAE reached around $904 million in 2005, which is about 42% higher compared to the previous year's figures.

701 | "Dubai is a booming and exciting industry to be a part of. The quality of the industry [advertising] is even developing. The reason why the industry is fast moving is due to the competitiveness in the market, whether it is in the fields of FMCG (Fast Moving Consumer Goods) or media. The variety of industries makes it a hub."
Chris Von Selle, Managing Director, *JWT*

702 | Advertising spend in the UAE's print media rose by 70%. Newspapers continued to generate the most revenue from advertising in Dubai and the UAE, worth $588 million in 2005 (65% of total advertisement spending), more than double the advertising value of $136 million generated by magazines (15%).

703 | Television won $133 million (14%) of advertising, and radio $7 million. Outdoor advertising in particular is booming, with real estate companies, trade fairs and multinationals boosting the growth in this sector. It accounted for $29 million of advertising spend in the UAE.

704 | "In the Gulf region, advertising expenditure grew 15% in 2005 to exceed $4.5 billion. By the end of 2006, advertising expenditure will exceed $5 billion. It will exceed $1 billion in the UAE and Saudi Arabia."
Khamis Mohammad Al Muqla, Bahrain Chapter President, *International Advertising Association*

705 | Dubai currently hosts more than 150 advertising firms, including regional offices of such household names as Saatchi and Saatchi, Leo Burnett, Impact BBDO and Grey Worldwide. More than 30,000 people work in the advertising and media sectors.

706 | "Dubai's media and advertising is fast climbing on to the world center stage. When a city, an economy, is headed for the limelight, media and advertising are almost inherently dragged up with it. You really cannot compare the scenarios in New York, London or say, LA to Dubai's. The challenges are different here, so the products are different. But with globalization playing an important part, you'll see a major positive shift in quality."
Fadi Salameh, President & CEO, *Promoseven*

707 | "If you are talking about attracting success, then I think that Dubai has done that. All the big boys are here. It's a city that is making a lot of noise and I think that's going to increase."
Vikram Naidu, Co-Chief Executive Officer, *Saatchi and Saatchi Middle East*

708 | "Dubai has the potential to emerge as a new global media and marketing hub."
David Domoney, Managing Director, *The Domus Group*

709 | "Dubai's marketing is fantastic and particularly strong in Europe. They keep announcing developments to keep people coming."
Gavin Samson, Associate Director, *TRI Hospitality Consulting*

710 | The direct marketing service sector in the UAE is expected to be generating incremental sales of approximately AED 47.7 billion ($13 billion) annually, with over 6% average yearly growth, according to Charles Prescott, Vice-President, International Business Development and Government Affairs of the Direct Marketing Association (DMA).

711 | "It's all very well bringing the world to Dubai, but who's going to bring Dubai to the world?"
Raja Trad, CEO for the Middle East and North Africa, Leo Burnett

TECOM |

712 | A subsidiary of Dubai Holding, The Dubai Technology & Media Free Zone (TeCom) is a tax-free commercial zone set up to support the development of knowledge based industries including the ICT sector, the media sector and companies that create and disseminate knowledge such as education and training institutions.

713 | TeCom estimated its expected investments in the field of communications abroad to register not less than AED 3.5 billion **($1 billion)** at the end of 2006, in terms of acquisition and purchase operations of world communication companies.

714 | TeCom manages the annual Dubai International Film Festival (DIFF), the IT Education Project (ITEP), an initiative that seeks to raise IT literacy in the UAE, Tamkeen, a training center for the visually impaired, and the UAE's leading radio networks.

715 | The Dubai Technology and Media Free Zone (TeCom) and Dubai Airport Free Zone (DAFZA) signed an agreement to collaborate in promoting excellence among companies in their zones. A "Benchmarking Partnership Team", set up by the 2 organizations aims to create the Dubai Learning Nucleus, a forum that will drive excellence among companies in DAFZA and TeCom by sharing best practices and learning opportunities.

Media & IT

INTELLECTUAL PROPERTY RIGHTS |

716 | The UAE has the lowest piracy rate in the region for the 10th consecutive year, and is the only Middle Eastern entry to the list of 20 nations with the lowest piracy rates. In fact, the UAE's piracy level of 34% is lower than that of several European countries, such as France, Italy, Spain, Portugal, Greece and Ireland, and is comparable to the piracy rates of the United Kingdom (27%), the Netherlands (30%) and Australia (31%).

717 | International organizations and institutions lauded the efforts made by the UAE to combat piracy and protect intellectual property rights and confirmed that the UAE has modern laws that protect copyright and intellectual property. Most notably the Arabian Anti Piracy Alliance and the US Consulate in Dubai also praised government departments and institutions for their efforts in rigorously enforcing the law and pursuing perpetrators of piracy crimes wherever they may be found.
Tamimi, Law Update newsletter

718 | The United Nations Conference on Trade and Development (UNCTAD) reports that the UAE continues to lead the region in protecting intellectual property rights (IPR). The report says both anecdotal and statistical evidence confirms that copyright, trademark, and patent laws are enforced.

719 | The Brand Owners Protection Group has been established and launched in Dubai, covering the Gulf region. The Group will seek to enforce existing intellectual property, copyright, patent and trademark protection and licensing laws in order to protect consumers from counterfeits and all other illicit trade, thereby defending the integrity of member organization brands.

720 | The founding members of the Brand Owners Protection Group include Beiersdorf, British American Tobacco, General Motors, Johnson & Johnson, Nestle, Philips and Unilever as brand owners and Al Tamimi & Co., Clyde & Co., Rouse & Co. International and Saba & Co. as service providers.

BUSINESS & RETAIL | 8

Business and Retail

In Dubai, retail business is black gold. 75% of the planned malls for the Gulf will be located in this Emirate. Fox News described Dubai as having "a New York business atmosphere and Cancun's tourism. Combine the two and you get Dubai. It is the hippest city in the world." Dubai has also been named the Middle Eastern City of the Future.
It's no wonder therefore that retailers, especially luxury brands, are attracted to this great city. It has a buzz and dynamism that makes both doing business and shopping fun.

"Dubai is an ideal venue for a debate on globalization. There's no place quite like it; it combines a vibrant cultural identity while playing host to a body of multi-cultural citizens. It is an important venue for global dialogue – a Davos with sand instead of snow – an ideal place to talk about globalization – a subject much discussed, but little understood."
HE Madeleine Albright, former US Secretary of State

OVERVIEW |

721 | "Not being well represented or based in Dubai means missing on current and future opportunities in the region".
Obaid Humaid Al Tayer, Chairman, *Dubai Chamber of Commerce and Industry (DCCI)*

722 | According to the results of Euromoney's country risk poll 2006, the UAE was ranked 29th globally, up from the 31st place it occupied in 2005. The UAE maintained its 1st place position in the Middle East and scored 78.63 points out of 100 regarding the country's stability in general, 19.3 points out of 25 regarding the political stability and 16.7 points out of 25 concerning economic performance. The country obtained a complete score vis-à-vis financial stability, bank financing performance and short term financial sources.

723 | Dubai presently accounts for over one-third of the region's total retail development.

724 | In a survey based on time, cost and effective facilitation for entrepreneurs in Dubai with regard to compliance with regulations in running their own enterprise, 80% or more of the 97 entrepreneurs surveyed, believe that it is easy to start a business and to get the right permits.

725 | "Dubai has now joined the ranks of Hong Kong, Shanghai and other rapidly growing areas. It is demonstrating enormous growth. The changes take one's breath away. Dubai's growth prospects seem truly unlimited. The architecture is dazzling. The innovation seems constant. It makes the imagination soar."
Steve Forbes, President and CEO, *Forbes Inc.*

Business & Retail

726 | "According to Labour Ministry figures, there are 250,000 businesses in the UAE that employ and sponsor about 2.4 million migrant workers from Asia."
Aisha Sultan, Deputy Head of the *government-sanctioned human rights association*

727 | Currently there is an extensive amount of new large-scale development in Dubai, related to both leisure and business, in both the public sector and the private sector at an estimated total cost of around $30 billion, according to a report released by HVS International.

728 | "Dubai's economy is expected to augment between 12% to 15% in tandem with nationwide growth. Dubai is implementing a number of strategic projects in order to sustain its competitiveness and leading position as a business hub. Over $100 billion worth of new ventures are either under execution or in the planning & approval phase."
Abdul Rahman Saif Al Ghurair, Vice-Chairman, *Dubai Chamber of Commerce and Industry*

729 | There are more than 250 commercial centers in the Middle East, including 40 malls in Dubai alone. The Emirate has 75% of the new malls planned in the Gulf region.

730 | "With Dubai attempting to rise as rapidly as possible up the value chain, the region is undergoing a tsunami of change."
Tom Peters, The Management Guru

731 | A recent international study on consumer confidence, conducted by ACNielsen by polling 23,500 internet users in 42 countries, revealed that consumers in Dubai and the UAE were optimistic about the future of the local economy, and were certain of an improvement of their financial circumstances and of better job opportunities.

732 | "Dubai is very accessible to Europe and other markets. It's globally competitive, and knows how to 'do global' really well. For a business to attract and be able to retain the best talent, you have to be in the best place, and I think for most international companies looking to establish themselves in the Middle East, it would be difficult for them to look past Dubai."
Lawrence Elms, Chairman, *Tejoori Investment Advisors* and Acting Chief Executive, *Tejoori Limited* and CEO, *DIFC*

733 | "I believe that Leaders in Dubai, which brings together some of the finest contemporary leaders in the world, offers a platform from which we can unite to deliver a message of hope. It can be a catalyst to further crystallize the mission our leaders must undertake and give it purpose and direction. The test of its success will be the outcomes we will see a year from now."

Mohammed Ali Alabbar, Director General, *Department of Economic Development of the Government of Dubai,* Chairman, *Emaar*

734 | Dubai was recognized as the 5th quality hub of the world and the headquarter of the Middle East Quality Association. This recognition for Dubai is a reflection of the emirate's commitment towards quality and also highlights the significant role played by the UAE and e-TQM College in propagating total quality management principles in the region.

735 | "Dubai's business environment is the Middle East's only meritocracy. Young men and women compete openly with ideas and ambitions to make their nation a model example for Muslim societies besieged by high unemployment, low literacy rates, bad trade policies and authoritarian political structures. They run businesses transparently, with integrity and with an increasingly democratic and accountable corporate culture."

Mansoor Ijaz, Chairman, *Crescent Investment Management*

RETAIL |

736 | "Those who are buying in Dubai are buying on trust."
Christopher Steel, Head of Middle East operations, *Hamptons International*

737 | According to Retail International, the total value of retail spend in Dubai is expected to touch $7.6 billion in 2009 and Abu Dhabi's retail spending will reach $1.9 billion, while Sharjah will cross $643 million. In total, retail spending in the UAE will reach almost $10.2 billion per year by 2009.

738 | The retail sector is boosted by the franchise sector of the UAE which is worth $14 billion and is believed to be growing by 27% a year, according to the UAE Yearbook 2005 in which fast foods comprise around 40% of the sector.

739 | "The new black gold discovered in Dubai is the retail business. Renowned world companies of luxury brands are betting on the fact that the local market will develop over the next 3 to 5 years. And in a decade, its size is expected to increase 3-fold."
Anji Shalhoub, President and Manager, *Etoile Collection*

Business & Retail

740 | "We like to be where investment is taking place and new traffic is going and this is one of the places where this is happening. It is hard to put a limit on this place. The excitement of this place is that you can try. Dubai's ability to attract high net worth individuals from all over the world and the travel retail customer in particular is an obvious attraction for luxury brands."
Ermenegildo Zegna, Owner, *Italian luxury menswear brand Ermenegildo Zegna*

741 | **IKEA,** a member of the Al Futtaim Group, expanded to a new 4-times-bigger-than-before store at Dubai Festival City (DFC). The 24,500 sq. m store, UAE's largest retail outlet, is the 1st retail outlet within DFC to be open to the public.

742 | **Al Futtaim** Technologies, a part of Al Futtaim Group's Electronics Division, has announced impressive growth of 41% in sales of 2005 as compared to 2004.

743 | French chain Carrefour is working with **Majid Al Futtaim (MAF)** and currently operates 8 stores in the country. MAF Group is expected to expand its shopping malls portfolio in the Gulf and beyond.

744 | **Al Tayer Group** plans to open 25 GAP and 10 Banana Republic stores by 2010 following the signing of a franchise deal with GAP Inc. The first GAP stores will open in late 2006 with Banana Republic stores scheduled for 2007. GAP Inc. signed a similar deal with partners in January to expand into Singapore and Malaysia.

745 | UAE Porsche dealer **Al Nabooda** Automobiles has clocked up 1,000 car sales in 2005, representing a 34% increase over 2004. This compares favorably to the average 500 units per year sold by the bigger Porsche centers in Germany, according to the General Manager Georg Brune.

746 | **Gargash** Enterprises, sole agents for Mercedes-Benz in Dubai and the Northern Emirates has increased its Passenger Car sales by a massive 30% over 2005. The Company publicly announced its target of selling 4,000 units in 2005, following a record breaking sales result in 2004.

747 | **Al Sayegh Brothers** has plans to increase its showroom and shop-in-shops from 16 in 2005 to 40 in 2008. The Group is the master distributor of LG Digital Products, Olympus, Palson and several other global brands in the UAE and declares that its turnover will grow by 25-30% per annum over the next 4 years.

748 | "It makes perfect sense to streamline our regional business geography and build our business from Dubai, where we will have a more regional focus and be able to mirror the needs of our multinational and regional client base."
Piyush Mathur, Regional Managing Director, *ACNielsen Eastern Europe, Middle East & Africa (EEMEA)*

749 | "Dubai's growing retail market driven by increasing numbers of overseas visitors is attracting more international investors. Like Singapore, Dubai has become known as a world-class shopping destination."
Tony Abdel Ahad, Director Retail Division, *Asteco*

750 | According to GODO Research Marketing Consultancy (GRMC), 50% of the UAE's retail activities are concentrated within hypermarkets.

751 | According to Retail International and Franchise.com, by 2009 retail activities in shopping centers would contribute about 50% to Dubai's GDP and the retail spending will shoot up to $3,500 per sq. m.

DUTY FREE |

752 | Ranked number 3 in the world in terms of turnover, **Dubai Duty Free** (DDF) has also seen an increase in the number of daily sales transactions, which now average **34,000** per day. The average value of each transaction has risen to $45 that is 3 times more than anywhere else in the world.

753 | Dubai Duty Free (DDF) reported sales of $590 million in 2005, which represents a 19% increase over the previous year. Sales continued their upward trend in the 1st quarter of 2006 as turnover reached $159 million representing a 12% increase over the same period 2005.

754 | Experts predict that Dubai free zone sales will reach $1 billion by 2008.

755 | Dubai Duty Free won the 'Best Airport for Duty Free Shopping' category for the 3rd consecutive year, by the Business Traveller UK magazine in 2006.

756 | As an example of Dubai Duty Free high transactions, it has the highest rate of Kit Kat

sales worldwide for an individual outlet with an equivalent sale of over 3,341 million Kit Kat four finger bars, equaling over 9,000 bars per day on average.

757 | Dubai Duty Free is the world's single largest Revlon cosmetics retail outlet. In 2005, sales of Revlon cosmetics at Dubai Duty Free increased by 42% to $1.1 million, making this the highest sales achieved worldwide from an individual store.

758 | Dubai Duty Free has successfully renewed its ISO 14001 certification and has simultaneously achieved OHSAS 18001, making it the 1st airport in the world and the 1st government department in the Middle East to hold both the environmental and health and safety certifications.

MALLS |

759 | Dubai, the official shopping hub of the Middle East, is also acknowledged as the core market for international retailers, prompting other Gulf countries to launch brands according to their success in this Emirate.

760 | There are several new shopping mall projects that are currently underway in the UAE and these malls will be mainly located in City of Arabia, Dubailand, Dubai Festival City, Dubai Outlet City, Burj Dubai Complex, Dubai Pearl Complex, and The Walk at Jumeirah Beach Residence.

761 | In early 2005, the total area of shopping centers in Dubai, was about 7 million sq. ft (or 6 sq. ft of retail outlet for every person). The ongoing and upcoming projects will increase this total area to 45.6 million sq. ft by 2010 (or 38 sq. ft for every person), more than double that of the US.

762 | Many reliable sources estimate that the visitors to Dubai's 25 major malls reached around 80 million in 2005.

763 | Dubai is the benchmark to judge all others. According to Retail International, at current demographic levels, the available retail facilities would require every man, woman and child in Dubai to spend $7,800 (AED 28,626) annually to sustain an overall average sales figure of $3,500 (AED 12,845) per sq. m a year in more than 25 shopping malls in Dubai.

764 | "Brands are coming to Dubai because it is a dynamic market. New malls will always be of interest to retailers."
Simon Thompson, Independent Retail Consultant, *Retail International*

765 | Deira **City Center** has long been the bustling heart of Dubai and has successfully maintained its position as the leading entertainment and leisure retail complex of its kind throughout the region. Home to over 300 shops, restaurants, cinemas and entertainment facilities, it continues to be a key destination and a focal point for the 60,000 shoppers who visit daily.

766 | In the 10 years since it opened its doors, Deira City Center has welcomed over 200 million visitors.

767 | "As of August 2005, 886,000 sq. m (Gross Leasable Area) shopping centers were completed in Dubai, while 874,000 shopping centers per sq. m (Gross Leasable Area) were still under development. Shopping center rental per sq. m was estimated at $70-75 per month."
Retail International / FDI Magazine

768 | Over 2005, **Burjuman** Center, one of the 1st major shopping malls in Dubai, witnessed expansions that multiplied its area by four and as a result its retail center occupies an area of 4.4 million sq. ft.

769 | Adding to its growing portfolio of industry awards, Burjuman was crowned Mall of the Year at the prestigious 1st Retail Middle East Awards, beating competition from malls across the region.

770 | In 2005, **Ibn Battuta Mall**, flung open its opulent new doors, with a design inspired by Andalusia, Tunisa, Egypt, Persia, India and China. The mall spreads across 3.5 million sq. ft including parking for 5,000 cars. The mall features a 21-screen megaplex, the region's first IMAX screen, 275 outlets, a food court across 3,800 sq. m and a Geant retail center covering 70,000 sq. m.

771 | The **Mall of the Emirates**, a retail entertainment and leisure resort, opened with 6.5 million sq. ft in total area and 2.4 million sq. ft in leaseable area.

772 | The largest shopping mall in the world outside North America is the Mall of the Emirates which has around 500 outlets, a ski resort, an Alpine-style hotel and a parking lot for

7,000 cars. The mall costs about AED 3 billion ($817 million) and is expected to see 30 million visitors every year. It was crowned the World's Leading New Shopping Mall at the World Travel Awards in London.

773 | "Our property is setting the standards for the retail industry across the UAE and the region. The customer traffic to our unique offering of leisure, shopping and entertainment has exceeded 10 million visits over the past 6 months and reflects the success of our business. The fact that we are exceeding our expectations as well those of our retailers is exciting and impressive."
Jim Badour, Vice President, *Mall of the Emirates*

774 | **Azal** Group, provider of retail and lifestyle franchises, has opened some of their signature outlets in the Mall of the Emirates, including Mango, Pull & Bear, Promod, Bershka, Sunglass Hut, Penny Black, Lanidor, Oysho, Paul, Columbus Café and Virgin Megastore, with a combined floor space of more than 152,000 sq. ft.

775 | The largest **Virgin** megastore in the Middle East is located in the Mall of the Emirates, offering 40,000 sq. ft dedicated to entertainment.

776 | **Harvey Nichols** has opened its largest store outside of the UK in Dubai's Mall of the Emirates. The store, designed by eminent architecture firm Callison Architecture, will span 3 levels and cover 136,900 sq. ft and will house more than 100 luxury brands managed by 409 professionals.

777 | **Tommy Hilfiger** Corporation, the $1.9 billion global apparel company, has launched its 1st UAE store at the Mall of the Emirates.

778 | Emaar's **Dubai Mall**, the AED 2.6 billion ($708 million) project lying at the heart of Burj Dubai, is the largest commercial center in the UAE. The mall will have 1,200 stores stretching over an area of about 12.1 million sq. ft including 3.7 million sq. ft of leasable space. Emaar expects the mall to attract about 35 million visitors per year. The mall will house 15 sub-malls, a skating rink, an aquarium and the planet's biggest gold Souq.

779 | The **Mall of Arabia**, due to open in 2008, will have 4 levels, around 1,000 outlets, its own theater and a parking for about 10,000 cars. The size of the mall will be over 10 million sq. ft of Gross Leasable Area (GLA) when completed, making it the world's biggest mall.

780 | Upon the completion of Dubai's Mall of Arabia and Dubai Mall along with the current

Mall of the Emirates and Ibn Battuta Mall, these 4 malls will be among the largest shopping malls in the world.

781 | **Dubai Outlet Mall**, spread over 4.3 million sq. ft is an integral part of Dubailand's AED 3.7 billion Dubai Outlet City (10 million sq. ft), it will be the 1st shopping mall for factory outlets in the region, housing the world's leading brands under one roof.

782 | Outlet Mall will have a gross leasable area of more than 1 million sq. ft and accommodate more than 200 outlets, a cinema complex, an amusement park and a parking for approximately 9,000 vehicles.

783 | Dubai Outlet City is to waive its sponsorship rights for international operators in a move that could render the UAE far more attractive for overseas businesses desiring to enter the GCC market.

784 | "Booming retail growth is directly tied to the rise in retail space in Dubai. This is in part due to the current boom in construction and development, which will see the Gulf countries close in on 12 million sq. m of gross leasable retail space before the end of the decade."
Mike Davidson, President, *Mideast Shopping Center Summit (MESCS)*

MICE |

785 | The Meetings, Incentives, Conventions and Exhibitions (MICE) sector is one of the essential contributors to Dubai's GDP.

786 | "Meetings and conventions contribute 40% to our tourism industry. We work to make every meeting, convention and conference a huge success and stay of the participants memorable."
Awadh Al Ketbi, Director, *Dubai Convention Bureau (DCB)*

787 | The **Dubai World Trade Center** (DWTC) has grown to be the most enduring corporate brand in the UAE. The 39-storey Trade Center Tower is one of Dubai's most recognizable icons. Its 239,000 sq. ft of high-end commercial space is occupied by a list of exclusive tenants, many of whom are world leaders in commerce and industry.

788 | DWTC is the premier venue for exhibitions and conferences in the Gulf and wider Middle

East region, offering 35,000 sq. m of prime exhibition space in various configurations in the Dubai International Convention and Exhibition Center (DICEC). DWTC will add an additional hall by September 2006, offering an extra 15,000 sq. m.

789 | Among the hundreds of yearly events in Dubai, DWTC alone is set to host a record 92 exhibitions in 2006 at its two venues, the Dubai International Convention and Exhibition Center **(DICEC)** and the Airport Expo – an average of nearly 2 events per week.

790 | "The number of international exhibitions the department participated in grew to 40 in 2005 (against the target of 31) from 24 in the year 2000. A feedback survey revealed that the success rate of Dubai's roadshows in 2005 was 99%. Over 98% of the participants expressed great satisfaction with the overall organization of the exhibitions in 2005, up from 86% five years ago."
Mohammed Khamis Bin Hareb, Director of Operations & Marketing, *Department of Tourism and Commerce Marketing (DTCM)*

791 | Dubai's expo sector, a major revenue earner for the Emirate, announced an AED 16 billion ($4.3 billion) redevelopment of the Dubai World Trade Center site that will house 40 skyscrapers when completed.

792 | "Recognizing the developing needs of the sector and the important growth opportunities that lie ahead, we have put two major stages of a strategic development plan in place to provide sufficient exhibition space for the future. The 1st stage is based upon expanding and enhancing the current exhibition space and facilities at DICEC to support the growth of the industry over the next 3 years. The 2nd stage will enable us to meet the exciting demands of the future, through the construction of Dubai Exhibition City, part of the Jebel Ali Airport City (World Central), by 2009."
Helal Saeed Al Marri, Director General, *DWTC*

793 | "I am a 6-time exhibitor at Gulfood and have had another successful year with 2 deals signed on the 3rd day, worth a total of $545,000."
Waiel Mansoor, Owner, *Jackson Vending Company*

794 | The professional expertise of DWTC staff and 1st class facilities has helped guarantee the success of a range of international exhibitions, including GITEX, the Middle East's largest and most important IT event, along with other major events like Gulfood, Big 5, CABSAT, Arab Travel Market (ATM), INDEX, Arab Health, Dubai International Boat Show and Dubai Motor Show.

795 | "Of the UK business travelers' favorite conference destinations, Dubai is the only long-haul destination in the top 10, according to Business Traveler International (BTI) UK."
The Guardian

796 | Dubai is one of the 8 members of the BestCities, the world's 1st and only convention bureau alliance. Its other members are Boston, Copenhagen, Edinburgh, Melbourne, Vancouver, Cape Town, San Juan and Singapore. The destinations represented by BestCities alliance partners have the facilities, attractions, and infrastructure to ensure a successful convention.

797 | "Dubai Chamber of Commerce & Industry is keen in developing the human resources, as it is an important feature for the success of an organization and the nation; this is achieved through providing scholarships, extensive training, seminars and courses pertinent to the development and performance of the employee."
Abdul Rahman Ghanem Al-Mutaiwee, Director General, *Dubai Chamber of Commerce and Industry*

798 | "Dubai is a great miracle."
Donald Trump, Chairman, President and CEO, *The Trump Organization*

TRADE & INDUSTRIES | 9

Trade and Industries

Dubai is the most significant international trading and economic hub in the Middle East. For instance, Dubai Logistics City (DLC) is the world's largest multi-modal logistics hub for air, sea and road services. Dubai Ports World (DP World), the region's leading port operator, recorded another year of impressive growth in container throughput for 2005, handling 7.62 million TEUs, representing 19% growth on 2004. To learn why Dubai is such an excellent trading hub, read this chapter.

"Dubai continues to expand its infrastructure to meet increasing demands & assert its position as the region's hub for trade and services."
Obaid Humaid Al Tayer, Chairman, *Dubai Chamber of Commerce and Industry (DCCI)*

OVERVIEW |

799 | Dubai, which has only modest oil reserves, has staked its future on an incredibly ambitious drive to be the region's leading commercial hub, a kind of Hong Kong on the shores of the aquamarine Gulf.

800 | Dubai has one of the most liberal trade regimes in the Gulf, and attracts strong capital flows from across the region.

801 | Dubai's role as a trading center has gained increasing importance due to its strategic geographic location, its extensive infrastructure facilities and the short turnaround time for cargo. The Emirate is a center for imports and re-exports from all major producers.

802 | "Dubai Chamber of Commerce & Industry plays a key role in supporting the business community and potential investors to develop, diversify their trade activities and interact with the business circles locally, regionally and internationally. Furthermore, Dubai has a strategic stance as a commercial and economic center conjugating many countries in the world with the biggest and most growing markets in the Middle East, Africa and Indian Sub-Continent, via numerous international trade fairs & exhibitions held in Dubai annually, conducive for business across the globe."
Abdul Rahman Saif Al Ghurair, Vice-Chairman, *Dubai Chamber of Commerce and Industry*

803 | Dubai boasts a sophisticated and world-class transportation infrastructure. Served by over 242 shipping lines and linked via 112 airlines to 165 destinations, Dubai's transport infrastructure is unrivalled in the region in terms of size, facilities and efficiency.

804 | "Commercial disputes, which may arise during business dealings, can be resolved through the Dubai International Arbitration Center (DIAC), using well developed procedures, which are equitable and cost-effective."
Dr. Hussam Al Talhuni, Director, *Dubai International Arbitration Center*

Trade & Industries

805 | "If any person wishes to access the UAE market, especially Dubai's, his products must be high quality so that they can compete with products from other countries... Hence, anyone who wants to be famous worldwide must be selling his products in Dubai."
Mohamed Anas Kuzbary, Member, Board of Directors, *Syrian Business Council in Dubai and Northern Emirates*

TRADE |

806 | In 2005, Dubai imported AED 207.6 billion ($56.5 billion), exported AED 44.2 billion ($12 billion) and re-exported AED 88.9 billion ($24.2 billion) according to the preliminary figures published by Ports, Customs and Free Zone Corporation.

807 | The UAE achieved a trade balance surplus of AED 163 billion ($44.4 billion) in 2005. Total exports hit a record AED 424 billion ($115.5 billion) while imports reached AED 261 billion ($71 billion).

808 | The UAE is a member of the Greater Arab Free Trade Agreement (GAFTA) which is supposed to come into effect by 2007.

809 | "Dubai Chamber of Commerce & Industry in partnership with "COFACE" launched Credit Rating initiation to facilitate the local and international business environments of its members through various value added products. COFACE alliance brings with it direct presence in 52 countries with local services offered in 92 countries."
Abdul Rahman Saif Al Ghurair, Vice-Chairman, *Dubai Chamber of Commerce and Industry*

810 | Trade made the largest contribution to Dubai's economy, accounting for 20% of its total GDP in 2004, and increasing by 110% compared to 2001.

811 | DCCI issued around 416,000 Certificates of Origin (COs) in 2005 covering export/re-export shipments of its members. Such shipments were worth AED 96 billion in 2005, representing 25% growth over the value of AED 77 billion recorded in 2004. The figure included exports/re-exports originating from Dubai and from the free zones, with the latter including those entering UAE's domestic market.

812 | "In 2005 the active registered members at Dubai Chamber of Commerce & Industry soared to about 57,420, a rise of 18.8% from 48,342 in 2004, the total escalation is about 130 times in four decades."
Abdul Rahman Ghanem Al-Mutaiwee, Director General, *Dubai Chamber of Commerce and Industry*

Trade & Industries

CITY OF GOLD |

813 | The World Gold Council regional office in Dubai announced that the UAE annual gold consumption in terms of sales increased 21% in 2005. The retail gold jewelry sales increased from AED 5.1 billion ($1.4 billion) in 2004 to AED 6.2 billion ($1.7 billion) in 2005.

814 | Dubai and the UAE are not only considered one of the largest consumers of gold, but also the 2nd import destination of Italian and Turkish gold jewelry after the US.

815 | "Dubai's gold imports were worth $10.7 billion in 2005 and they will double in 5 years."
Jeffrey Rhodes, General Manager, *Standard Bank*

816 | Dubai imported 522 tonnes of gold in 2005, up from 503 tonnes in 2004 and 373 tonnes in 2003. About 170 tonnes were sold in the local market in 2005, of which 70 tonnes were locally processed.

817 | According to a recent report by GFMS (Gold Fields Mineral Services) world gold supply averaged 3,997 tonnes in 2005, which means that one in every 8 tonnes of gold supplied in the world comes to Dubai.

818 | At present, Dubai's gold retail trade is worth over $3 billion and is an important contributor to UAE's GDP, making Dubai a growth-oriented market. Dubai also has the largest per capita consumption of gold.

819 | "This is the world's fastest growing jewelry market and is set to double its retail space in the next 4 years."
Tawhid Abdullah, Chairman, *Dubai Gold and Jewelers Group (DGJG)*

820 | 95% of the tourists who visit Dubai during the Dubai Shopping Festival (DSF) buy gold. The establishment of gold refineries and the Dubai Gold Receipt have enhanced the image of Dubai internationally and made Dubai a mature market with international standards.

821 | Dubai's jewelry retail trade stands at $1.5 billion out of which $408 million is in diamond jewelry alone.

Trade & Industries

822 | The total trade in rough diamonds in Dubai jumped 46.25% in 2005, to $3.734 billion, up from $2.553 billion in 2004. Dubai exported diamonds valued at $2.248 billion in 2005 while imports for the same period touched $1.484 billion.

823 | According to latest statistics, 25-30% of rough diamonds produced in the world pass through Dubai before heading to their final destinations. Furthermore, it's estimated that 94% of Dubai's rough and polished diamond imports are re-exported.

824 | "The Middle East, where gold and jewelry trade is expected to grow manifold in the coming years, does not have a center and we believe that Dubai could match the likes of London, New York and Hong Kong and become an international industry hub."
Dr. Gaetano Cavalieri, President, *World Jewelry Confederation*

E-COMMERCE |

825 | "In 2005 Dubai Chamber of Commerce & Industry launched Dubai Trade Point – an affiliate of the World Trade Point Federation. This innovative E-Commerce service is a strategic initiative to create global opportunities for the business community in Dubai."
 Majed Hamad Al Shamsi, Vice-Chairman, *Dubai Chamber of Commerce and Industry*

826 | **Tejari**, is the Middle East's premier online business-to-business marketplace that allows companies to buy and sell goods and services online. Its trade volume exceeded $2.8 billion in 6 years. Tejari launched mylinkDubai.com for all businesses and companies registered with the Dubai **Department of Economic Development** (DED).

827 | "DED's mission is to expand the scope of commerce in Dubai and mylinkDubai offers a compelling e-commerce proposition for organizations from every industry, regardless of size. We anticipate that organizations will embrace mylinkDubai and gain significant new business opportunities within the first six months of activating their membership."
Ali Ibrahim, Deputy Director-General, *Dubai Department of Economic Development (DED)*

828 | "The volume of e-trade in the first quarter of 2006 stood at $200 million. We expect that the value of operations would attain $1 billion by the end of 2006, with a growth rate of 25% compared with 2005."
Omar Hijazi, Chief Executive Officer, *Tejari*

Trade & Industries

FOREIGN TRADE |

829 | Dubai imports more than two-thirds of the UAE's needs, as well as part of the needs of the GCC markets annually.

830 | "Dubai is at the forefront of trade in the region, and the establishment of specialized free zones and economic clusters have effectively positioned Dubai as the hub of trade to the vast markets of the AGCC, Middle East, North Africa and the subcontinent."
HE Sheikha Lubna Bint Khalid Al Qasimi, UAE Minister of Economy and Planning

831 | "Dubai is an important international trading and economic hub; it enjoys excellent bilateral ties with more than 165 countries. It is a dream destination for investors across the globe, providing a conducive investment and business environment, no taxation and with political, economic, and social stability."
Abdul Rahman Ghanem Al-Mutaiwee, Director General, *Dubai Chamber of Commerce and Industry*

832 | According to the latest available statistics, China ranked first in the amount of imports to Dubai in 2004, valued at $5 billion, while exports amounted to $62 million.

833 | "In 2005, trade between China and the UAE was AED 39 billion ($10.7 billion), making it China's 2nd biggest trading partner in the Gulf after Saudi Arabia whose trade touched AED 58.72 billion ($16 billion). Our trade with the UAE grew by 32% in 2005 over 2004 and due to the robust economic development in both countries in recent years, we expect to maintain 30-40% growth in the coming years."
Cao Jiachang, Representative in the Department of West Asian and African Affairs, *Ministry of Commerce in China*

834 | The UAE is India's largest trade partner in the Middle East with its imports accounting for $7.1 billion in 2004-2005 period. The UAE is also India's 3rd largest trade partner after the US and China. India ranked 1st among the top 20 countries for Dubai's exports and re-exports in 2004, recording $574 million and $3 billion respectively. The country also ranked 2nd in Dubai's imports with $4.8 billion.

835 | "Of the total mutual trade, $2.5 billion constitutes Iran's exports to Dubai with $7.5 billion going to imports from Dubai, while over 25% of Iran's trade is carried out via Dubai. Iran's re-exports from the Emirate totaled $2.8 billion and ranked 2nd after India. Also, UAE exports to Iran have increased 65% in this period."
Massoud Mirzaei, Iran's Commercial Attache in Dubai and Head of *Iran Trade Center in Dubai*

Trade & Industries

836 | Trade between the UAE and Pakistan totaled $2.78 billion in 2005.

837 | Dubai is now the UK's 10th largest export market in the world. Trade statistics released by the UK's Department of Trade and Industry show that exports to Dubai rose by 134% in 2005, reaching a total value of AED 30.9 billion ($8.4 billion).

838 | "According to DCCI, trade (including oil and free zones trade) between the UAE and 14 EU countries continued to accelerate between 2004 and 2005. Based on EUROSTAT trade statistics, EU15's total trade with the UAE in 2005 reached EUR 33.9 billion, increasing by 48% over the corresponding figure of EUR 22.9 billion in 2004. Although the trade balance continued to be in favor of EU15, EU15's imports from the UAE grew by a hefty 85% in 2005, reaching EUR 9.7 billion, while exports to the UAE grew more slowly at 37% to reach EUR 24.2 billion."

Abdul Rahman Ghanem Al-Mutaiwee, Director General, *Dubai Chamber of Commerce and Industry*

839 | The USA ranked 2nd in Dubai's exports and 4th in Dubai's imports with $138 million and $2.5 billion respectively in 2004. Trade between the USA and the UAE increased to AED 36.5 billion ($9.95 billion) in 2005 compared to AED 19.2 billion ($5.2 billion) in 2004, according to the US Department of Commerce. The UAE was the largest export market of the US in the GCC. Of the AED 70 billion ($19 billion) exports to the GCC in 2005, 44% was destined to the UAE.

840 | Dubai's position as a significant port of entry for products destined to GCC markets is reflected in the volume of exports that flow from Dubai to the GCC markets. In 2005, about 44% of Dubai's exports/re-exports covered by certificate of origins (COs) were shipped to GCC markets, with Saudi Arabia cornering the largest share.

841 | A free trade agreement between the UAE and Australia is likely to be concluded by mid 2006. Australia's exports to the UAE, during the first three quarters of 2005 reached almost AED 2.5 billion ($681 million), while imports from the UAE amounted to AED 771 million.

842 | Japan reported a 31.7% increase in its total trade with the UAE during 2005, for a total value of AED 111 billion ($30.2 billion). In 2004, Dubai's imports from Japan reached $2.8 billion while Dubai's exports amounted to $85.6 million.

843 | "With the bilateral trade between UAE and South Korea amounting to over AED 36.7

Trade & Industries

billion ($10 billion) up to October 2005, there is a strong indication that the end year figures would exceed AED 44 billion ($12 billion). In 2004, the bilateral trade between the 2 countries stood at AED 36 billion ($9.8 billion.)"
Hee-Beom Lee, Minister of Commerce, Industry and Energy, *Republic of Korea*

844 | Electronics have always been one of Dubai's attractions for shoppers. There are more than 500 electronic product types that Dubai deals in. Electronics sales in the Dubai domestic market reached AED 8 billion ($2.18 billion) in 2004, a 23% increase from 2002 figures. Dubai's total imports of electronics reached $4.4 billion in 2004 and re-exports recorded a total of $2 billion, excluding imports and re-exports from free zones.

845 | The textile market in the Middle East has continued its strong growth in 2005, with total trade through Dubai touching an astonishing AED 21.5 billion ($5.8 billion), an increase of 15% over 2004, according to trade traffic statistics compiled by the Statistics Department of Dubai Ports, Customs and Free Zone Corporation (PCFC).

846 | "The office furniture market in the UAE is estimated to be between AED 700 million and AED 1 billion, and the carpets and flooring another AED 1 billion."
Ajai Dayal, General Manager of Retail and Marketing, *Easa Saleh Al Gurg Group*

DP WORLD |

847 | "The tremendous success and growth of our port business in recent years has led us to make significant changes to the organization of the whole Dubai Ports group. DP World combines the strengths of both DPA and DPI legacy organizations to create a very powerful global player in the ports operator industry. In addition, the creation of a new regulator and a new combined free zone operator puts in place a more effective and focused overall organization."
Sultan Ahmed Bin Sulayem, Chairman, *Dubai Port World*

848 | Dubai Ports, which comprises **Dubai Ports Authority** (DPA and DP World), has been at the forefront of Dubai's extraordinary transformation into one of the world's leading trade and commerce hubs. DPA is focused on the home ports at Rashid and Jebel Ali which DPI formed in 1999 (as **Dubai Ports International**) to export this success internationally. DPI initially applied its expertise to managing ports in the Middle East, India and Europe.

Trade & Industries

849 | In the shipping world, Dubai Ports enjoys a solid reputation as one of the Middle East's most successful companies. With its emphasis on services, Dubai has become a thriving trade center not only for the Gulf but for Asia as well.

850 | Dubai Ports World (DP World), the region's leading port operator, recorded another year of impressive growth in container throughput for 2005, handling 7.62 million TEUs (Twenty-foot Equivalent Units/Containers), which represents 19% growth for 2005 compared with 2004.

851 | A few years ago, the idea of ships carrying 6,000 TEUs was a jaw dropper. Today, the previous amount seems relatively small when compared to the 8,000 TEUs ships that sail today. By the year 2030, DPA will have a handling capacity of 55 million TEUs a year.

852 | Dubai Ports Authority (DPA), one of the fastest-growing ports in the world, has won the "Best Seaport Award in the Middle East" for the 11th consecutive year at the Asia Freight and Supply Chain Industry Awards (ASFCA) 2005.

853 | "DP World is amongst the foremost global marine terminal operators with a strong focus on meeting our customers' needs and surpassing their expectations. The continued growth at our home ports of Dubai reflects the success of this approach." **Jamal Majid Bin Thaniah,** Vice Chairman, *Ports & Free Zone Authority*

854 | DP World's AED 25 billion ($6.8 billion) acquisition of the Peninsular and Oriental Steam Navigation Company (P&O) completed the global geographic chain for Dubai Ports, filling in the missing link to North America. The combined group would have a capacity of 50 million TEUs across 51 terminals in 30 countries, including the 6 at issue in the US.

855 | DP World is ranked the 7th largest container terminal operator worldwide by throughput, while its flagship facility of Port Rashid and Jebel Ali in Dubai are together ranked 9th, according to industry newsletter Dynaliners.

856 | Dubai Ports, the fastest growing operator in the world, witnessed more than 25% average growth in container traffic during the past 4 consecutive years, while the air cargo increased 40% during the same period.

857 | "DP World-UAE continues to be at the forefront of implementing new technologies,

Trade & Industries

and has further enhanced security at its terminals. Jebel Ali Terminal recently made heavy investments in the infrastructure systems and handling equipment in order to expand its capacity and increase service levels. It is the first and only user in the region of the new super large container cranes which can simultaneously lift two 40 ft containers or four 20 ft containers over a ship at one time, significantly improving efficiency."
Mohammed Al Muallem, Senior Vice President and Managing Director, *DP World*

DUBAI LOGISTICS CITY |

858 | "The Supply Chain & Logistics organizations in Dubai contribute up to 8% to the Emirate's GDP, as Dubai attracts business volumes comparable to other known cities. Dubai has been known as a major center for re-export since the 60s, thanks to the vision of Dubai Rulers who made Dubai an international business hub that competes with Hong Kong & Singapore and is the 3rd player in the field of shipping, export and re-export."
Majed Hamad Al Shamsi, Vice-Chairman, *Dubai Chamber of Commerce and Industry*

859 | Dubai Logistics City (DLC) is the world's 1st and largest integrated multi-modal logistics platform for air, sea and road services. DLC, is part of the 140 sq. km Jebel Ali Airport which is 5 times bigger than Frankfurt cargo.

860 | "Dubai Logistics City is delivering a dream concept of an integrated logistics platform as it seamlessly integrates with the new international airport in Jebel Ali and the existing Jebel Ali Port and Free Zone for air and ocean transport infrastructure. In Europe, we missed the opportunity for such a platform and now there is no such expansive land available for integration of transport modes and logistics businesses."
Dr. Hans-Peter Stabenau, Head of *the German Logistics Academy of Bremen*

861 | When completed, Dubai Logistics City will cover more than 25 sq. km and handle more than 12 million tonnes of air cargo every year through 16 air cargo terminals. Work on the new runway began in October 2005 and was scheduled to be fully operational by 2007. This runway will be capable of handling the new generation of A380 airliners.

862 | Around 50 companies, one of which is the world's 10th largest logistics company, Kuehne & Nagel, are getting ready to construct facilities in Dubai Logistics City. This is part of the 1st phase of the gigantic World Central, an area reaching 140 sq. km.

Trade & Industries

863 | "We have a huge demand for Dubai Logistics City (DLC) by well known international companies. More than 50% of the land has been already booked."
Tarik H. Shalabi, Senior Manager, Finance and Administration, *Department of Civil Aviation (DCA)*

864 | "All these companies have bought into the DLC value proposition of being centered in the world's first truly integrated logistics and multi-modal platform which is being created by DLC, Jebel Ali Port and Free Zone and the new international airport at its core. All these clients understand the sheer business viability of locating to a hub which can serve a geographic footprint of over 2 billion consumers all within 2 to 3 hours flying time of Jebel Ali."
Michael Proffitt, Chief Executive Officer, *Dubai Logistics City*

865 | Cargo mega terminal will have the capacity to handle 5 million tonnes of freight by the year 2018.

866 | In March 2005, global logistics firm DHL announced a joint venture with the Dubai customs authorities that would see the creation of an electronic customs clearance system designed to streamline procedures and improve general business efficiency in the UAE and beyond.

867 | "The e-clearance project resulted in the complete digitisation of all customs clearance procedures which intended to reduce shipment transit times by up to 24 hours. By implementing this new procedure, DHL UAE is helping Dubai increase its customs efficiency which will, as a direct knock on effect, increase productivity for regional businesses and customers."
Derek Tully, Manager, *UAE Customs and Gateway*

868 | ARAMEX, the leading provider of total transportation solutions in the MENA region and South Asia, unveiled its state-of-the-art logistics facility at Jebel Ali Free Zone. The AED 26 million center is built on a land area of 430,000 sq. ft.

869 | "This Jebel Ali facility is a very important milestone in our plan to build an advanced logistics infrastructure which is a continuation of our global expansion strategy. The facility is designed to play an integral part in facilitating commerce in the region by creating solutions capable of adapting to the constant changes in the global trading system."
Fadi Ghandour, Chief Executive Officer, *ARAMEX*

DUBAI MARITIME CITY |

870 | Dubai Maritime City (DMC), spread across 216 hectares, is located on a man-made peninsula between **Port Rashid** and the **Dubai Dry Docks** and is surrounded by the waters of the Arabian Gulf. When completed, DMC will be the world's biggest and the most comprehensive maritime complex and will expand the scope of business for nearly 5,000 major regional maritime companies already operating in Dubai.

871 | DMC will provide a strategic location for 7 main sectors: maritime management, maritime services, maritime retail & recreation, maritime education & research, ship repair & maintenance, yacht repair & maintenance and yacht manufacture. The first phase of the project will be ready for occupation by the end of 2006.

872 | Since its establishment in 1979, **Jadaf Dubai** (Dubai Ship Docking Yard), the Arabian Gulf's oldest ship repair and industrial marine yard, has emerged as the preferred dock for prominent fleet operators such as Seabulk International, Amasco, Al Jaber, Stanford Marine, Gulf Agency, Inchcape, NMS and Inter Marine, besides attracting customers from South Asian, African and European countries.

873 | Jadaf Dubai has recorded a 35% jump in revenues for the year 2005, compared to 2004. The yard's 2 docks repaired and carried out maintenance of a total of 2,347 ships during 2005 as compared to the 2,181 vessels it catered to during 2004. Jadaf Dubai also serves various kinds of seafaring vessels in partnership with 275 companies operating within the yard and another 150 companies dealing with the yard externally.

874 | "The completion of Jebel Ali Port's 1st expansion phase, scheduled for the 1st quarter of 2007, will result in a 20% increase in trans-shipment handling and a 16% rise in imports and exports. The developments taking place at Jadaf Dubai, Dubai Dry Docks and the completion of Dubai Maritime City in 2006 will be a tremendous boost to the Emirate's maritime industry."
Jamal Majid Bin Thaniah, Vice Chairman, *Ports, Customs and Free Zone Corporation (PCFC)*

875 | Jadaf Dubai has been named the number 1 ship docking yard in the world by Rolls Royce Naval Marine Company, for completing over 59,100 operations on a variety of vessels. This recognition highlights Jadaf Dubai's commitment to providing the highest quality ship docking operations to regional and international clients.

Trade & Industries

INDUSTRY OVERVIEW |

876 | "Dubai is the showcase for the Middle East, Africa and the Indian sub continent."
Obaid Humaid Al Tayer, Chairman, *Dubai Chamber of Commerce and Industry (DCCI)*

877 | Dubai's industrial sector grew by 15% in 2005 and reached around $5 billion, tripling in just one decade.

878 | According to the latest Emirates Industrial Bank report, with a rapidly expanding non-oil economy growing at an average of 23% in the past 5 years, industrial investments in the UAE have grown fast with the number of units now at 3,294 employing 245,707 people.

879 | The investments made in the UAE's manufacturing sector recorded AED 70 billion ($19 billion) in 2005, representing an increase of 8.4% from 2004. UAE's manufacturing sector accounts for 19.2% of the GDP, positioning itself as the 2nd largest contributor to the national economy.

880 | "We have noticed that the Dubai government seems to be very interested in industry, particularly because we have found Dubai willing to grant industrial licenses faster than anywhere else in the region. It has a good industrial infrastructure with ports and other facilities as well as an adequate commercial climate".
Dr. Ahmad Al Mutawa, Secretary General, *Gulf Organization for Industrial Consulting*

881 | At the GCC country level, UAE ranks 2nd in the plastic industry after Saudi Arabia. The most produced plastic products pipes and household products. According to DCCI membership database, locally there are 119 establishments manufacturing plastic and rubber products in Dubai with a turnover of AED 1.3 billion ($354 million) by the end of 1st quarter 2006.

882 | The national pharmaceuticals industry meets only 20% of the UAE demand with 80% met by imports. The latter shows the significance of domestic market opportunities in the UAE.

883 | The petrochemical industry in the UAE has grown tremendously in the last decade. The value of investments in the sector in 2005 totaled AED 15 billion ($4 billion), representing 22% of the total manufacturing investments in the UAE.

Trade & Industries

884 | UAE's food and beverage industry attracted investment worth AED 31.2 billion ($8.5 billion). The sector was the largest in terms of investment within the manufacturing sector with 299 industries accounting for the largest portion of the AED 414 billion ($112.8 billion) investment (46% of total investment).

885 | The Dairy & Fruit Juice industry registers 10% annual growth in Dubai and meets 56% of local demand.

DUBAL |

886 | **Dubal**, a 100% Dubai government-owned entity and one of the largest single site aluminium smelters in the western world is the industrial flagship of Dubai. The company produces and exports high quality, value added primary aluminum products to more than 40 countries worldwide. Dubal also contributes more than **7%** to Dubai's GDP.

887 | The multi-billion dollar state-of-the-art Dubal complex comprises a 761,000-tonne capacity primary aluminium smelter, a 1,750 MW power station, a large carbon plant, 3 casthouses, a 30-million gallon per day desalination plant, laboratories and research facilities, a sea port, storage facilities, maintenance areas and administration buildings.

888 | Dubal consolidated its position as a major force in the world aluminium industry, reporting a 10% increase in net profits for 2005 following a 14% surge in sales.

889 | Costing over AED 1 billion ($272 million), Dubal's new enlargement project offers additional productive energy reaching 100,000 tonnes of aluminum and, in return, the overall productive energy will increase to 861,000 tonnes. The giant company is also planning a 25% increase of the production capacity of its Jebel Ali smelter by 2010, to more than 1 million tonnes annually.

890 | The UAE unveiled plans for what will be the world's largest single-site aluminium smelter with a capacity of 1.2 million tonnes per year (tpy). The $6 billion smelter complex will be built at Taweelah in Abu Dhabi following a joint development agreement, signed between Mubadala Development, an investment arm of the Abu Dhabi government, and Dubal.

891 | "Dubal has already spent more than AED 1 billion to maintain and continuously

Trade & Industries

upgrade its systems to create better environment standards. During the start up of Potline 7B, DUBAL was able to benchmark and align its environmental standards with globally accepted regulations."

Abdullah Bin Kalban, Chief Executive Officer, *Dubal*

DUBAI INDUSTRIAL CITY |

892 | Dubai Industrial City, an industrial zone clustering manufacturing facilities in high value added sectors from the UAE, GCC and Far East regions, will sprawl across 560 million sq. ft of prime land. The city will concentrate on 6 manufacturing sectors, machinery & mechanical equipment, transport equipment, base metals, chemicals, food and beverage and mineral products.

893 | "Dubai Industrial City will be one of the active drivers that will catalyze foreign direct investment (FDI) and attract new technology and technical expertise. We estimate that over the next 5 years, Dubai Industrial City will easily be able to attract AED 4-5 billion in industrial investment."

Khalid Al Malik, Chief Executive Officer, *Dubai Industrial City*

894 | The Dubai Industrial City will establish '**Maqayees**' Dubai Center for Industrial Standards, which will set the operational performance standards for industries and related institutions operating from the city. 'Maqayees' Dubai Center for Industrial Standards will embark on branding the Dubai Quality Mark™ as an integral standard encompassing and broadening the requirements of various international management system standards like ISO 9000, ISO 14000, ISO 18000 and HACCP complemented with a risk assessment and rating model.

895 | Al Wasit Machinery, a leading UAE national-owned company specializing in construction and heavy machinery equipment, is setting up one of the region's 1st construction equipment assembly plant in Dubai Industrial City. The plant is to be located at the City's Transport Equipment and Parts Zone and will cover an area of almost 1 million sq. ft.

DUBAI TECHNO PARK |

896 | Dubai Techno Park is the leading local economic zone in the Middle East and a member of the International Association of Science Parks (IASP). The focus of the Park is in 3 key areas: hi-tech, oil and gas and desalination and water technologies. While these 3 sectors form the primary focus, Techno Park also welcomes companies oriented towards other advanced technologies.

897 | "Dubai Techno Park is a world-class industrial complex and a center for hi-tech manufacturing for local and international companies. Techno Park is located in the heart of Dubai's industrial zone, and offers facilities and services comparable to the best in the world, making it an ideal investment destination."
Abdullah Ahmed Al Qurashi, Chief Executive Officer, *Dubai Techno Park*

898 | Dubai Techno Park has so far incorporated 75 companies as part of its 1ˢᵗ phase. Meanwhile, applications for another 55 companies are under process. The park has already leased out over 90% of its phase one and 25% of its phase two developments. In addition, the park authorities are negotiating with around 1,000 companies globally that might be willing to join the park.

Trade & Industries

INVESTMENTS & COMPANIES | 10

Investments & Companies

An increasing number of companies are setting up in Dubai because of its fast-track processing and registration of businesses. JAFZA hosts around 5,000 companies of which more than 2,000 are multinationals and 140 are Fortune Global 500 companies. The rush to establish a presence in Dubai is due to its strategic location, the unparalleled incentives and services offered, and the dynamic business community.

On a larger scale, with no barriers to entry and no foreign exchange controls, the UAE attracted $18 billion of foreign direct investment in 2005. The outlook is promising for the coming years.

"Dubai is seeking weapons of mass economics. The ease of money transfer in terms of free movement of capital by foreign investors in the country at any time sets a good example of the bureaucratic system developed here. Dubai, as a re-export hub, should be regarded as the region's gateway to international markets since it already has a strong and safe infrastructure for the re-export industry."

Lieutenant General Dhahi Khalfan Tamim, Commander-in-Chief of *Dubai Police* and Chairman of the Board of Directors of *Juvenile Association*

OVERVIEW |

899 | "The UAE received $18 billion in foreign direct investment (FDI) in 2005, double the previous year. The country will remain attractive to international investors since it allows 100% foreign ownership in the free trade areas."
HE Sheikha Lubna Bint Khalid Al Qasimi, Minister of Economy and Planning

900 | The models used in Dubai demonstrate that investment is the underlining factor for the Emirate's growth. At the end of the 1990s, investment was impressive, with an equilibrium annual investment rate of 25% between 1985 and 2003 and an average growth of capital stock between 1993 and 2003 of 9.9%. This means that recorded levels are sustainable and tend to exceed the equilibrium level at times.

901 | There are 20 free zones that play a major role in attracting investments to Dubai and there are another half-a-dozen free zones underway. These free zones constitute a vital part of the local economy, as well as a main regional hub covering the GCC region.

902 | Venture Capital and private equity are an integral part of a robust financial sector. The private equity in UAE increased by $2 billion by the end of 2005.

903 | "We, in Dubai, are in the heart of the world. We get the ideas and experience (on rules of arbitration) from every part of the world; from UK, Singapore, USA, Hong Kong and France. We'll have our own rules of arbitration very soon."
Dr. Husam Al Talhuni, Director, *Dubai International Arbitration Center (DIAC)*

Investments & Companies

904 | As further recognition of Dubai's ever increasing rate of expansion and level of sophistication, the Chartered Institute of Arbitrators has approved the establishment of a UAE branch in Dubai for its members.

905 | "Dubai promotes a secure, attractive environment for foreign investment. It eliminates the red tape that slows business. It creates incentives for young entrepreneurs including women. It invests in infrastructure and it creates a tourism industry that attracts millions of travelers, some of whom like the country so much they consider locating businesses here."
The New Republic

906 | "We will develop 17 of our brands in Dubai alone, in one of the largest new mass initiatives of the group. Dubai is growing exponentially."
Donald Trump Junior, Vice President for Development & Acquisition, *The Trump Organization*

907 | The Growth Competitiveness Index, released by the World Economic Forum, ranks the UAE as the 5th worldwide in the macroeconomic management index, after Singapore, Norway, Denmark and Finland.

908 | Family companies represent nearly 92% of the privately held companies in the UAE. The Dubai Chamber of Commerce and Industry (DCCI) has statistics indicating that there are 56,374 companies operating in Dubai, including 30,769 family businesses.

909 | "We have high expectations. We know we are in the right place and with the right people."
Assaad Jabre, Executive Vice President, *International Finance Corporation*

INVESTMENTS |

910 | UAE attracts more than 25% of foreign direct investment in the GCC.

911 | Dubai Investments is a world-class company that invests in viable and profitable entities. It is the largest investment company listed on the Dubai Financial Market. Its prudent use of capital and sound management skills enables it to establish, acquire, or strategically participate in successful corporate ventures throughout the region.

912 | "In 2005, Dubai Investments registered profit growth of 116% to reach AED 666 million

Investments & Companies

($181 million), compared to AED 309 million in 2004. The company's overall income increased 69.4% to reach AED 1.525 billion against AED 900 million in 2004. Total assets reached AED 3 billion in 2005 compared to AED 2.25 billion the previous year, a 34% increase. The return on capital increased from 43% in 2004 to 78% in 2005."
Khalid Bin Kalban, Managing Director and Chief Executive Officer, *Dubai Investments*

913 | Dubai Investments has reported exceptional results for the first quarter of 2006, with consolidated total income of AED 460 million ($125 million), which is 103% more than the total income of AED 227 million ($61 million) for the same period in 2005. The net profit for the period was AED 253 million ($69 million), which is 360% more than the net profit of AED 55 million for the same period in 2005.

914 | **Dubai Investments Park** (DIP) is a subsidiary of Dubai Investments and a major industrial, business, residential and recreational development. DIP's major attraction for investors is the long-term leases, renewable up to 99 years that are available for industrial, commercial and residential projects. The park consists of 4 business zones including the Industrial Zone, Commercial Zone and the Residential and Recreational Zone. It also hosts leading international schools, thus making it like a mini-educational zone.

915 | **M'SHARIE**, a wholly owned subsidiary of Dubai Investments, currently has a portfolio of 13 companies including Emirates Extrusion Factory, Gulf Dynamic Switchgear , Lite Tech Industries, Gulf Metal Craft, Metrofile, Labtec, Gulf Dynamic Services, Emirates Explosives, Emicool, Syscom Emirates, Thermoset Technologies, National Insulite and Emirates Thermostone.

916 | "We plan to invest about AED 5 billion ($1.36 billion) in 2006 and 2007. At least AED 1.5 billion ($408.7 million) will be invested in real estate projects and the rest in industrial and other investments."
Khalid Bin Kalban, Managing Director and Chief Executive Officer, *Dubai Investments*

917 | "Dubai Chamber of Commerce & Industry is a key player in enhancing the economic activities in Dubai, constantly supporting the competitive business environment and providing investment opportunities, enabling them to interact with local, regional and international business circles.
Majed Hamad Al Shamsi, Vice-Chairman, *Dubai Chamber of Commerce and Industry*

Investments & Companies

918 | "Dubai seems to be pursuing a strategy of brand development. It is different from other Gulf countries."
Ali Shihabi, Chief Executive Officer and Founder, *Rasmala Investments*

919 | "Foreign direct investment (FDI) in the UAE is picking up and we have identified the potential of companies like ours. There is enormous investment potential in Dubai and our global track record will ensure a safe financial environment for our investors."
Frank Simon, General Manager, *Trend Capital*

920 | More and more, Dubai is becoming home to the regional head offices of international firms such as Microsoft Corporation, DaimlerChrysler and Oracle Corporation.

921 | "At the moment there are increasing investments from South Africa in Dubai and the UAE. I think that is due to the attractive investment climate in the UAE as well as the return on investments (ROIs). Dubai and the UAE are South Africa's largest trading partner in the GCC."
HE Ismaeel Obaid Yousef Al Ali, UAE Ambassador to South Africa

922 | International Finance Corporation (IFC), the private sector arm of the World Bank Group and the Mohammed Bin Rashid Establishment for Young Business Leaders have decided to form a partnership to promote entrepreneurship programs in the UAE. This partnership aims to increase awareness and demand for Small and Medium Enterprises (SMEs) management training amongst entrepreneurs and SMEs in the UAE.

923 | "The presence of some of the world's and the region's most respected and prestigious businessmen and women in Dubai will inspire the business ambitions of the young Arab community and fuel sustainable growth. This will benefit the individuals, their immediate environment and, ultimately, the region."
Abdul Baset Al Janahi, CEO, *Mohammed Bin Rashid Establishment for Young Business Leaders*

924 | "It is a tremendous opportunity to expand in Dubai and be part of substantial regional growth."
Simon Cooper, Chief Operating Officer, *Ritz-Carlton Hotel*

925 | **Al Mal Capital**, a Dubai-based investment company, launched an AED 1 billion equity fund that is projected to earn an annual return of 25-30% over a 3-year period. Targeted at high net-worth and institutional investors, the Al Mal UAE Equity Fund is designed as an institutional product with a minimum subscription of AED 1 million per investor.

Investments & Companies

926 | **Abraaj Capital,** the largest private equity firm in the Middle East, North Africa and South Asia region, has been voted "Middle East Private Equity Firm of the Year" by readers of the Private Equity International (PEI) magazine from around the world. The award marks a year of significant achievement for Abraaj Capital that closed the region's biggest ever fund, the Abraaj Buyout Fund II, at $500 million. It also manages investments for the Abraaj Buyout Fund I, the Abraaj Special Opportunities Fund and the Abraaj Real Estate Fund.

DUBAI ABROAD |

927 | The **Dubai Investment Group** was honored for its investment dealings in one of the world's most sophisticated financial markets by winning the prestigious "US Hotel Deal of the Year" award from America's Lodging Investment Summit (ALIS). The group is the world's leading hotel industry association and Dubai Investment Group was named for its deal in acquiring the landmark New York Essex House Hotel in September 2005.

928 | **In its 1st year of operation, Dubai International Capital (DIC), a member of Dubai Holding:**
   • Invested $1 billion (AED 3.67 billion) in DaimlerChrysler, making DIC the company's 3rd largest shareholder.
   • Committed over $300 million (AED 1.1 billion) to private equity funds.
   • Made a $1.4 billion (AED 5 billion) acquisition of The Tussauds Group in the UK, the largest operator of visitor attractions in Europe.
   • Invested $272 million (AED 998 million) in Jordan Dubai Capital which targets opportunities in Jordan.
   • Became an anchor investor in Ishraq, a $150 million (AED 550.5 million) company formed to develop and own up to 22 Express by Holiday Inn hotels in the Middle East.
   • Made a $1.2 billion (AED 4.5 billion) acquisition of Doncasters, a leading manufacturer of precision engineered components and systems for applications in aerospace, industrial gas turbines, automotive turbocharger and medical technologies sectors.

929 | "A $12-$15 billion investment fund has been set up by Dubai International Capital Company to buy shares of Fortune 100 companies. The fund is expected to begin operating by the end of the 2nd quarter of 2006. The company would pay in $200-$300 million as the lead investor in the fund, which would also have institutions, large family groups and government investment authorities of several countries as subscribers."
   Sameer Al Ansari, Chief Executive Officer, *Dubai International Capital*

Investments & Companies

MULTINATIONAL |

930 | Dubai and the UAE are home to the largest number of Chinese companies among the GCC states. There are 2,000 Chinese companies operating in the UAE and the trade exchanges reached $10 billion between both countries.

931 | "China is seeking to leverage Dubai's status as the business hub of the MENA, India and the subcontinent."
Hao Feng, Chairman, *Chinamex Middle East Investment & Trade Promotion Center*

932 | Currently, there are over 500 Dubai-based German companies operating in the UAE with total investments of around $40 million. Non-oil trade between Germany and the UAE increased in last few years and reached $5.1 billion in 2005.

933 | The UAE and Dubai in particular, continue to attract a large number of British firms aiming at doing business in the region. One of Dubai's main attractions is that it is perceived as a stepping-stone to launching businesses across the UAE, the wider Gulf region and North Africa.

934 | "I'm very optimistic about the UK-UAE and UK-Dubai business relationships. I think we will continue to see more trade and investment in both directions. This is partly because Dubai is seen, and is used, by British companies as a regional hub and not just as a market in its own right. British companies find Dubai a very good place to do business, and they find it an easy place to set up. They find it has a fantastic logistics center and that the access to the region is excellent."
John Hawkins, Consul General, *British Embassy in Dubai*

935 | "Due to its stability and security, the UAE is becoming an important destination for Belgian companies which are increasing their presence, almost on a monthly basis."
Mohammad Al Rashedi, UAE Chargé d'Affairs in Brussels

936 | "Dubai in particular, among the seven UAE Emirates, has become a business partner for many American companies in recent years, as it expands its international airline, creates a major financial center and stock exchange, and adds to its already substantial hotel and tourism business."
The New York Times

937 | Many American companies are making enormous profits as a result of the prosperity

Investments & Companies

Dubai is witnessing. Among these companies are Sun Microsystems, IBM and construction companies such as Parsons, Bechtel, Turner and architectural companies such as Skidmore Owings and Merrill.

938 | "We are very pleased that Dubai Holding has agreed to work with us in growing the infrastructure and industrial sectors across the region. This understanding will ensure that the most advanced technology in the world will be deployed here with the most optimum means of financing to be facilitated by Dubai Holding and GE's Capital Markets - Corporate group. The track records of both our companies in development efforts in the region are impressive and our partnership aims to build on them."
Jeffery Immelt, Chairman and CEO, *General Electric*

939 | "The UAE remains one of the most strategic markets for American Express Middle East. The company has heavily invested in expanding operations there as well as getting the adequate resources on board. We are determined to continue investing in building our UAE business in the future."
Prem Patel, Marketing Director, *American Express Middle East*

940 | The number of Italian companies operating in Dubai, according to the DCCI membership database, reached 111 companies in 2005.

941 | Dubai Chamber of Commerce and Industry's (DCCI) database show that the number of Australian companies operating in Dubai has witnessed a significant increase in the year 2005, bringing the total number of companies to 139.

942 | Around 150 Belgian companies operate in the UAE.

JAFZA |

943 | "JAFZA is the perfect example of the power of partnership, combining the technical and marketing expertise of our highly professional team with your business acumen. Local support and market knowledge are essential, combined with excellent infrastructure, ease of procedure and attractive incentives."
Sultan Ahmed Bin Sulayem, Executive Chairman, *Ports, Cutoms and Free Zone Corporation*

944 | JAFZA is a free zone that provides companies with all the assistance they require to set up and operate within Dubai's encouraging environment. As one of the largest

Investments & Companies

and fastest growing free zones, Jafza offers its customers world-class infrastructure supported with quality, value-added services and incentives.

945 | Today, JAFZA hosts around 5,000 companies, more than 2,000 multinational companies. 140 Fortune Global 500 companies have taken advantage of the strategic location, incentives and services offered by JAFZA.

946 | "JAFZA still attracts lots of international blue chip companies."
Salma Hareb, Chief Executive Officer, *Jebel Ali Free Zone Authority (JAFZA)*

947 | "Statistics issued by Dubai Chamber of Commerce & Industry indicate that the Government of Dubai has invested recently $2.5 billion in projects to develop the Free Zones and Jebel Ali port, which would draw a large number of Global Operations, holding renowned trademarks. As the Free Zones constitute around 5,000 companies, representing approximately 100 countries, offering jobs to 100,000 workers, the number of industrial facilities operating in the Free Zones attained 512 facilities in the first half of 2005."
Abdul Rahman Saif Al Ghurair, Vice-Chairman, *Dubai Chamber of Commerce and Industry*

948 | There are more than 588 Indian companies at JAFZA, which is 11% of the total companies located in the zone.

949 | "Japanese companies traditionally have chosen JAFZA as their operations hub for the Middle East. Presently there are over 90 Japanese owned companies operating out of JAFZA including prestigious names such as Bridgestone, Sony, JVC, Kenwood, Hitachi and Honda."
Ibrahim Al Janahi, Vice President, *Jebel Ali Free Zone Authority*

950 | "Jebel Ali is a logistics hub for Toshiba as our products manufactured in Singapore, Thailand, Japan and Indonesia are routed through the free zone for regional distribution. The extremely high purchasing power, the growing interest in new products, and increased awareness levels among customers in the region cemented our decision to base our regional headquarters here in Dubai."
Yasuyoshi Matsunaga, Managing Director, *Toshiba Corporation*

951 | Examples of more international companies operating in JAFZA as a regional hub: Black and Decker, Komatsu, Cussons, Colgate-Palmolive, Nestle, HJ Heinz, Unilever, Nivea, L'Oreal, BP, Total, Shell, BASF, Tata, Nissan, Mitsubishi, Bridgestone, Acer, Bose, Sanyo, Yamaha, Matsushita, Philips, Siemens, Nokia, DaimlerChrysler, Swarovski and others.

Investments & Companies

AUTO |

952 | Based on Dubai's vision to be a regional center, Jafza & Business Parks Management announced the establishment of **Dubai Auto Zone** as the future primary market place for the Auto industry. The AED 2 billion ($545 million) project, due to be completed by the end of 2007, will facilitate traders, light manufacturers, service providers, and others in the automotive and machinery industry.

953 | Dubai Auto Zone will consist of a Free Zone to attract foreign direct investment, a Specialized Economic Zone to cater to the GCC market, and a Retail Zone to serve the local market.

954 | "The purpose is to create a specialised marketplace for the automobile business. We hope to have manufacturers, traders, suppliers and end-users in one place."
Hamza Al Haddad, Marketing Vice President, *Jafza*

955 | The **Dubai Cars and Automotive Zone** (DUCAMZ), managed by the Jebel Ali Free Zone Authority, was established with the objective of re-exporting cars to Asia and African region where the demand for vehicles exist and continues to grow. The zone comprises one million sq. m of bonded area.

956 | Dubai Ports, Customs and Free Zone Corporation (PCFC) figures show that trade in automobile spare parts through Dubai recorded 40% growth in 2005 over the previous year. Between 2000 and 2005, the auto spare parts trade in Dubai increased by 155%. The total value of vehicle spare parts trade in 2005 was more than AED 18 billion ($4.9 billion) compared with AED 13 billion ($3.5 billion) in 2004.

OUTSOURCE |

957 | "Outsourcing is a very fast growing business globally. We anticipate 40% annual growth in this field."
Ahmad Bin Bayat, Director General, *Dubai Technology, Electronic Commerce and Media Free Zone Authority (TeCom)*

958 | The 1st phase of **Dubai Outsource Zone** is targeting a 5% share of the global outsourcing industry. It will have 250,000 sq. ft of rentable area off the Emirates Road. The 2nd phase of the project, which is seeking to have between 200 and 300 companies in 5 years.

Investments & Companies

time, will add another 200,000 sq. ft and is scheduled for completion by early 2007.

959 | "We are not trying to compete with India, we are trying to complement it. No one will refuse to come. Dubai could be 20% more expensive, but you could get more productivity."
Ismail Al Naqi, Director, *Dubai Outsource Zone (DOZ)*

960 | Dubai Outsource Zone (DOZ), which is set to be run as a completely private unit, is expected to generate 40-50,000 jobs in the next 5 to 7 years before breaking even in about 12 years.

HEALTHCARE |

961 | **Dubai Healthcare City (DHCC),** a $1.8 billion project, will be the biggest center for medical and healthcare on an international level within the area between Europe and the South East. All DHCC partners share the goals of creating patient-centered care, making healthcare accessible to all and creating and nurturing a community of porfessionals.

962 | "Our aim at Dubai Healthcare City (DHCC) is in line with the goals of the Ministry of Health, which are to support and to develop the medical sector in the UAE. The vision and strategy of DHCC is offering state of the art healthcare services in the region."
Saeed Al Muntafiq, Chief Executive Officer, *Tatweer*

963 | Among the leading academic medical institutions and preeminent healthcare organizations who have joined DHCC: Harvard Medical International, Mayo Clinic, Astrazeneca, Johnson & Johnson, American Academy of Cosmetic Surgery Hospital and Novo Nordisk.

964 | Harvard Medical School Dubai Center (HMSDC), an institute for Postgraduate Education and Research, is being set up by the Harvard Medical College and is opening in 2006.

965 | By partnering with Harvard Medical School, Dubai Healthcare City hopes to create a global center for treatment, education and research. DHCC which will begin operating in 2009, sprawls across 4.5 million sq. ft. The next phase will cover an area four times as big.

Investments & Companies

966 | "People who needed treatment had to pick up and leave. They had to go to Europe, they had to go to the United States, and they had to go to Asia. This really is making a statement that you no longer have to go. We have the best of the world here."
Ahmad Sharaf, Chief Executive Officer, *Dubai Energy*

DUBIOTECH |

967 | Dubai Biotechnology and Research Park (DuBiotech) is intended to be the hub and the center of excellence in the region since it is the first and only one of its kind in biotechnology.

968 | DuBiotech has two main areas of interest. The first is the Foundation for Research & Innovation (FRI), which will be the main arm focusing on government-funded R&D. The second aims to set up a biotechnology industry cluster with the appropriate infrastructure, facilities and services for incubators, R&D labs, biotech-related educational institutions, suppliers and manufacturing companies.

969 | Dubai Biotechnology and Research Park (DuBiotech) has signed a memorandum of understanding (MoU) with the Frankfurt Biotechnology Innovation Center. The agreement sets the framework for joint work in life sciences research, education, professional training, and also the development of marketable products in the health sector.

970 | "With this cooperation, we will expand our worldwide network and secure further access to research knowledge and emerging markets. The cooperation with DuBiotech represents a great opportunity for German and European enterprises in the sector of life sciences and healthcare to open up new markets in the Middle East and will enable them to bring together resources for groundbreaking and profitable projects."
Dr. Christian Garbe, Managing Director, *Frankfurt Biotechnology Innovation Center (FIZ)*

DUBAI HUMANITARIAN CITY |

971 | **Dubai Aid City (DAC)** provides international aid organizations with a hub from which to organize humanitarian efforts. It offers facilities to store and distribute aid cargo to destinations throughout the world and to conduct their governance and co-ordination activities.

Investments & Companies

972 | **Dubai Humanitarian City** is an initiative focused on facilitating humanitarian efforts on a global platform.

973 | In October 2005, Dubai Holding and the Ports, Customs and Free Zone Corporation announced the agreement to merge Dubai Aid City (DAC) and Dubai Humanitarian City (DHC) creating the biggest aid facilitator of the region, located in Jebel Ali Free Zone. The new non-profit entity will provide a full resource center for international regional and local relief and development organizations and UN agencies.

FLOWER |

974 | Strategically located at Dubai International Airport, the **Dubai Flower Center** (DFC) is set to become the new hub of growth for the floriculture industry in the 21st century. The 34,000 sq. m facility is designed to handle more than 180,000 tonnes of flowers and other horticultural perishables per annum.

975 | When fully developed, Dubai Flower Center will have a floor area of approximately 100,000 sq. m and a handling capacity of 300,000 tonnes of product per annum.

976 | DFC will ensure that produce arrives at its destination as fresh as the day it was harvested. It has been designed as a fast-moving trans-shipment hub, enabling the floriculture industry to improve quality and grow profits through cost-effective logistics.

977 | According to Interflora Dubai, the Emirate imported 150 kg of flowers per week on average in 1999. In 2005, imports increased considerably to 10 tonnes per week, with 5 million flowers being sold in the UAE over the year.

978 | "Dubai Civil Aviation has invested about $70 million in the Dubai Flower Center at Dubai International Airport. By routing goods through tax-free Dubai, shippers can save time and money in the delivery chain connecting more than 15 producing countries with Asian, African and Middle Eastern markets."
Michael Mueller, Managing Director, *Planetfair Dubai*

979 | "GCC countries imported more than 30,000 tonnes of plants and flowers in 2005. Around 50% of that was imported by the UAE alone. With rising demand from hotels, government authorities, private buyers and mega real estate projects, we estimate this industry segment will experience significant regional growth."
Egon Gallinis, Managing Director, *Messe Essen GmbH*

Investments & Companies

DUBAI IS NOT A DREAM ...

980 | **The First Arab Business Intelligence Report 2005, based on a survey of 140 prominent Arab leaders in the financial services, healthcare, travel and tourism sectors, and carried out by Moutamarat and PricewaterhouseCoopers, presents the following results:**
- 38% of the leaders surveyed indentify the UAE as a specific growth market across all sectors.
- 74% of surveyed executives in the travel and tourism sector consider the UAE as having a reputation for good customer service.
- 56% of surveyed senior executives in the financial services sector believe that the UAE will be home to the region's most prominent stock exchange in 3-5 years time.
- 63% of UAE businesses are seeking alliances and joint ventures.

981 | "A successful case study like Capital Partners has already encouraged American firms to look to the UAE for investment opportunities. With all of the right mechanisms in place, including the support for private sector initiatives, high levels of transparency, and a commitment to FTA initiatives, American companies will set up operations here."
W. Jonathan Wride, Managing Director, *Capital Partners*

982 | "Dubai is booming and opportunities are mushrooming everywhere. The city is giving birth to its new entrepreneurs and attracting more from the region and the far corners of the world. Locally incorporated businesses are expanding and growing phenomenally."
Hashim Al Dabal, Chief Executive Officer, *Dubai Properties*

983 | "Sheikh Mohammed's ultimate goal is to put Dubai in the ranks of the greatest cities of the world and it's quickly becoming a New York, Paris, Tokyo or Chicago. But whereas those cities took hundreds of years, this city took 25 years."
Franko Vatterott, Owner, *Human Interest Group*

984 | "People think it is a dream, but people are wrong. What we start here, we finish."
Khaled Issa Al Huraimel, General Manager, *Madinat Al Arab Project*

Investments & Companies

TESTIMONIALS ...

985 | **Time :** Dubai's economy is the healthiest in the Middle East.

986 | **Newsweek :** It's an open city for an open world.

987 | **The New York Times** : Dubai's unofficial motto is: the bigger and brasher, the better.

988 | **The Washington Post :** An ambitious city that caters to tourists rather than terrorists in a country where the motto should be, "Over the top is not nearly high enough."

989 | **Financial Times :** In its bid to become the business capital of the Middle East, Dubai already has purpose-built business parks for most sectors of the economy.

990 | **The Economist :** Arabia's field of dreams, Dubai is one of the world's most successful business ventures; a small city that learned lessons from Singapore and Hong Kong.

991 | **The Independent :** It is the fastest growing city on earth.

992 | **BusinessWeek :** Dubai's dramatic new developments won't be without their critics. Love them or hate them, these new wonders of the world are just that… wonders.

993 | **The Korea Times :** "You cannot live here without reading newspapers everyday." This is how they describe the rapid changes taking place in Dubai.

994 | **The New Republic :**   Dubai does everything the Arab world doesn't – and it could serve as a lesson to its larger neighbors.

995 | **FDI Magazine :** Politically stable, Dubai has a forward-looking, responsive government with a progressive, pro-business attitude and a strong commitment to the private sector.

996 | **Forbes :** Dubai is a place where the act of moving around sand dunes always involves billions of dollars.

Investments & Companies

997 | **Wall Street Journal :** Dubai has aggressively leveraged its role as a crossroads to develop a diversified economy.

998 | **Vanity Fair :** Las Vegas is a sputtering 20-watt bulb compared with this fire in the desert.

999 | **The Times :** Dubai is where imagination knows no boundary. It is a place unfettered by limitations of money, space and ambition. Its skyline and shoreline change daily.

1000 | Please go to Quotation number one.

Investments & Companies

Indicators

2004 - 2005

All the tables in this section are taken from the "2004 Statistical Yearbook - Emirate of Dubai" (16th Edition, October 2005) and "Dubai in Figures - 2005" published by the Dubai Municipality, Statistics Center, and some tables are from the Dubai Department of Civil Aviation.

Dubai Quarterly Statistics 2005

Demographic & Vital Statistics - 2005				
	Q1	Until Q2	Until Q3	Until Q4
Total Population in (000)	**1,086**	**1,101**	**1,116**	**1,130**
Male	803	816	829	841
Female	283	285	287	289
Total Births*	**3,223**	**6,392**	**9,435**	**12,640**
Male	1,694	3,330	4,855	6,507
Female	1,529	3,062	4,580	6,133
Total Deaths*	**383**	**792**	**1,117**	**1,520**
Male	294	575	815	1,123
Female	89	217	302	397
Married Cases	582	1,146	1,682	2,216
Divorced Cases	160	304	473	625

*Excluding Private Sector
Source: Dubai Municipality
        Health & Med. Services Dept.
        Dubai Courts Dept.

Building & Construction - 2005				
	Q1	Until Q2	Until Q3	Until Q4
No. of Completed Building	**588**	**1,158**	**1,762**	**2,252**
Commercial	103	192	265	333
Residential	387	775	1,210	1,529
Recreational/Services/Industrial	98	191	287	386
Value of Completed Building (in Million 000 AED)	**1,415.5**	**3,235**	**5,095.7**	**7,873.5**
Commercial	765.8	1,436.6	2,227.3	3,849.2
Residential	432.9	928.5	1,503.0	2,111.9
Recreational/Services/Industrial	216.8	871.4	1,365.4	1,912.4
Land Transaction				
Number	1,486	2,948	3,907	4,880
Value (in Million AED)	7,935	18,029	26,458	32,628

Source: Dubai Municipality
Land Department

Transportation & Communication - 2005				
	Q1	Until Q2	Until Q3	Until Q4
Air Transport				
Total Aircrafts at Dubai International Airport	52,738	105,646	159,738	217,165
Passengers Movement at Dubai International Airport (000)	**6,026**	**11,837**	**18,527**	**24,782**
Departure Passengers (000)	2,857	5,692	8,816	11,811
Transit Passengers (000)	224	432	657	860
Arrival Passengers (000)	2,945	5,713	9,054	12,111
Marine Transport				
Passengers Movement at Dubai International Ports	**15,992**	**30,779**	**51,560**	**70,602***
Arrival	8,134	15,380	26,733	36,412*
Departure	7,858	15,399	24,827	34,190*
Vessels Calling to Dubai International Ports	7,912	16,775	25,445	34,572
Public Transportation				
No. of Buses	446	416	422	458
No. of Lines	69	62	64	70
No. of Passengers (000)	20,683	41,504	62,620	84,268

* Including Jebel Ali port in Q4
Source: Department of Civil Aviation
　　　　Dubai Municipality
　　　　Naturalization & Residence Department of Dubai
　　　　Dubai International Ports

Hotels & Tourism - 2005				
	Q1	Until Q2	Until Q3	Until Q4
Hotels				
No. of Hotels	281	288	292	300
No. of Rooms	27,438	28,194	28,999	29,808
No. of Guests	1,347,655	2,619,865	3,982,275	5,294,485
No. of Guestnights	3,527,550	6,672,877	10,052,942	13,375,784
Bed Occupancy rate	87.3%	85.2%	77.3%	76.7%
Hotel Apartments				
No. of Hotel Apartments Bldgs.	98	98	100	106
No. of Flats	7,534	7,625	7,464	8,305
No. of Guests	205,565	403,228	637,506	865,518
No. of Guestnights	715,010	1,379,827	2,179,321	2,928,703
Flat Occupancy rate	83.8%	79.0%	83.1%	75.5%

Source: Department of Tourism & Commerce Marketing

Finance & Business - 2005				
	Q1	Until Q2	Until Q3	Until Q4
Dubai Financial Market				
Trading Value (Million Share)	3,277	9,793	17,973	25,542
Trading Value (Million AED)	38,165	165,564	306,307	405,162
Number of Executed Deals	156,169	546,500	1,160,021	1,734,497
Market Capitalization (AED Mn)	181,009	523,926	926,135	1,332,998
Licenses				
Commercial Licenses				
New (Issued)	2,389	5,045	7,324	9,492
Renewed	9,643	17,018	22,200	27,607
Modified	5,172	13,885	22,041	30,436
Cancelled	342	703	980	1,268
Professional Licenses				
New (Issued)	486	1,026	1,500	2,068
Renewed	3,230	5,866	7,778	9,600
Modified	1,086	3,519	5,777	8,147
Cancelled	138	313	412	528
Industrial Licenses				
New (Issued)	56	131	176	231
Renewed	361	668	881	1,086
Modified	163	464	749	1,031
Cancelled	8	14	19	24
Tourist Licenses				
New (Issued)	70	141	224	298
Renewed	203	379	515	654
Modified	149	329	500	713
Cancelled	0	1	7	8
Intelaq Licenses				
New (Issued)	57	124	188	260
Renewed	25	52	87	119
Modified	19	55	77	93
Cancelled	19	29	43	54
Certificates of Origin issued	**98,155**	**203,229**	**308,398**	**418,002**

Source: Dubai Financial Market
Department of Economic Development
Dubai Chamber of Commerce & Industry

Dubai Direct Trade During - 2005* (Value in Million AED)		
Import	Export	Re-Export
207,629	44,197	88,900

Source: Ports, Customs & Free Zone Corporation
* Preliminary Figures

Electricity & Water - 2005				
	Q1	Until Q2	Until Q3	Until Q4
Generated Electricity (G.W.H)	3,047	8,101	14,637	19,327
No. of Consumers	288,735	297,280	301,794	308,616
Quantity of Water production (million gallons)	13,284	28,673	44,949	60,624
No. of Consumers	235,162	242,148	246,540	252,012

Source: Dubai Electricity & Water Authority

Telecommunication - 2005				
	Q1	Until Q2	Until Q3	Until Q4
No. of Telephone Lines & Fax Lines	496,504	503,547	511,716	520,249
No. of Mobile Telephone Lines	1,572,123	1,647,950	1,734,612	1,833,940
No. of Telex Lines	544	529	523	518
No. of Internet Lines	149,119	152,542	156,166	162,846

Source: Emirates Telecommunication Corporation

Vehicles Recorded by type - 2005			
	Q1	Until Q2	Until Q3	Until Q4
Light Vehicles				
New	27,826	57,641	93,107	136,902
Renewed	69,162	122,518	184,726	261,504
Light Buses				
New	834	1,910	3,088	4,306
Renewed	1,642	3,208	6,580	8,440
Heavy Buses				
New	669	1,134	1,841	2,571
Renewed	1,246	2,349	2,425	4,120
Light Trucks				
New	2,618	5,371	7,719	7,811
Renewed	8,595	15,781	26,924	27,266
Heavy Trucks				
New	1,429	3,087	4,243	5,613
Renewed	3,973	7,039	7,505	11,794
Light Mechanical Vehicles				
New	162	436	754	994
Renewed	395	795	2,172	2,710
Heavy Mechanical Vehicles				
New	478	1,015	1,501	2,069
Renewed	1,048	1,889	1,959	3,259
Light Tankers				
New	-	21	28	29
Renewed	15	26	71	81
Heavy Tankers				
New	68	132	221	224
Renewed	388	685	1,028	1,057
Light Refrigerating Trailors				
New	74	126	168	172
Renewed	251	477	702	705
Heavy Refrigerating Trailers				
New	6	55	66	124
Renewed	66	114	122	540
Motorcycles				
New	538	1,125	1,731	2,583
Renewed	902	1,559	2,233	3,029

Source: Dubai Police General Head Quarters

Passenger Movement - Passenger - 2005				
Year	Uplifted	Discharged	Transit	TOTAL	inc/dec%*
2001	6,188,467	6,212,394	1,107,212	13,508,073	9.64%
2002	7,376,965	7,522,283	1,074,143	15,973,391	18.25%
2003	8,523,354	8,651,712	887,278	18,062,344	13.08%
2004	10,296,963	10,572,393	842,527	21,711,883	20.21%
2005	11,811,383	12,110,909	859,996	24,782,288	14.14%

* Comparison % with previous year
Source: Deparment of CIvil Aviation

Cargo Movement - Freight (Tonnes) - 2005			
Year	Uplifted	Discharged	TOTAL	inc/dec%*
2001	261,214	349,653	610,867	8.6%
2002	338,788	425,405	764,193	25.1%
2003	430,240	510,355	940,595	23.1%
2004	508,699	602,948	1,111,647	18.2%
2005	622,979	710,035	1,333,014	19.9%

* Comparison % with previous year
Source: Deparment of Civil Aviation

Aircraft Movement - Aircraft - 2005				
Year	Scheduled	Non-Sched.	Military	TOTAL	inc/dec% *
2001	114,052	15,069	5,044	134,165	-5.0%
2002	123,193	20,533	6,118	149,844	11.7%
2003	141,766	21,292	5,453	168,511	12.5%
2004	166,537	24,663	4,620	195,820	16.2%
2005	180,947	30,621	5,597	217,165	10.9%

* Comparison % with previous year
Source: Department of Civil Aviation

Passenger - 2005

Year	Uplifted	Discharged	Transit	Total	inc/dec%*
1994	2,583,158	2,616,595	1,099,426	6,299,179	11.0%
1995	2,923,052	2,967,012	1,212,920	7,102,984	12.8%
1996	3,479,777	3,434,676	1,094,115	8,008,568	12.7%
1997	3,873,938	4,105,170	1,129,658	9,108,766	13.7%
1998	4,286,069	4,416,578	1,029,555	9,732,202	6.8%
1999	4,831,879	4,886,486	1,036,459	10,754,824	10.5%
2000	5,516,621	5,600,146	1,203,893	12,320,660	14.6%
2001	6,188,467	6,212,394	1,107,212	13,508,073	9.6%
2002	7,376,965	7,522,283	1,074,143	15,973,391	18.3%
2003	8,523,354	8,651,712	887,278	18,062,344	13.1%
2004	10,296,963	10,572,393	842,527	21,711,883	20.2%
2005	11,811,383	12,110,909	859,996	24,782,288	14.1%

* Comparison % with previous year
Source: Department of Civil Aviation

G.D.P. at Factor Cost in year 2004*
(Million AED at Current Prices)

sector	%		Value	
	Dubai	U.A.E	Dubai	U.A.E
Non-Oil G.D.P	40.7	100	103,954	255,500
Gross Domestic Product	100	100	110,654	378,761
The Non Financial Corporations Sector	85.78	86.78	94,919	328,702
Agriculture, Live Stock & Fishing	0.74	2.67	818	10,100
Mining and Quarrying				
Crude Oil and Natural Gas	6.05	32.54	6,700	123,261
Quarrying	0.08	0.22	91	828
Manufacturing Industries	14.6	13.08	16,159	49,546
Electricity, Gas & Water	1.47	1.77	1,628	6,720
Construction	12.18	7.52	13,474	28,468
Wholesale, Retail Trade and Repairing Services	19.96	10.21	22,084	38,682
Restaurants & Hotels	3.79	1.94	4,189	7,343
Transports, Storage & Communication	13.69	7.2	15,149	27,263
Real Estate & Business Services	10.6	7.8	11,724	29,540
Social & Personal Services	2.62	1.83	2,903	6,951
The Financial Corporations Sector	9.49	5.89	10,498	22,318
Government Services Sector	6.91	8.5	7,645	32,201
Domestic Services H.H	0.55	0.56	616	2,126
(Less) Imputed Bank Services	2.73	1.73	(3,024)	(6,586)

*Preliminary data

Of Per Capita G.D.P. at Current Prices in 000 AED (Estimated)	103.3

Source: Dubai Municipality, 2004 Statistical Yearbook, Emirate of Dubai

Gross Domestic Product By Economic Sectors - DUBAI
(Milion AED)

SECTORS	2000	2001	2002	2003	2004*
The Non Financial Corporations Sector:	**51,681**	**54,188**	**67,876**	**83,167**	**94,919**
- Agriculture, Live Stock and Fishing	501	525	544	571	818
- Mining and Quarrying :	6,443	5,142	5,003	5,281	6,791
* Crude Oil and Natural Gas	6,365	5,068	4,926	5,198	6,700
* Quarrying	78	74	77	83	91
- Manufacturing Industries	10,090	10,538	11,794	13,986	16,159
- Electricity, Gas and Water	1,031	1,080	1,392	1,431	1,628
- Construction	5,066	5,218	8,870	11,961	13,474
- Wholesale Retail Trade and Repairing Services	10,163	10,517	14,618	19,950	22,084
- Restaurants and Hotels	2,713	2,977	3,243	3,639	4,189
- Transports, Storage and Communication	8,047	10,211	11,783	13,817	15,149
- Real Estate and Business Services	6,057	6,290	8,333	9,784	11,724
- Social and Personal Services	1,570	1,690	2,296	2,747	2,903
The Financial Corporations Sector	**6,187**	**7,517**	**7,992**	**9,321**	**10,498**
Government Services Sector	**5,659**	**5,939**	**6,600**	**7,305**	**7,645**
- Domestic Services of Households	475	567	598	598	616
Less: Imputed Bank Services	1,667	2,183	2,572	2,648	3,024
TOTAL	**62,335**	**66,028**	**80,494**	**97,743**	**110,654**

*Preliminary data
Source: Ministry of Planning

Dubai Emirate - Workers by Economic Sectors Emirate of Dubai - (Worker)					
SECTORS	**2000**	**2001**	**2002**	**2003**	**2004***
The Non Financial Corporations Sector :	**435,840**	**504,677**	**637,210**	**718,706**	**767,524**
- Agriculture, Live Stock and Fishing	7,640	9,557	9,645	10,538	10,987
- Mining and Quarrying :	3,830	4,378	4,556	4,790	5,270
* Crude Oil and Natural Gas	3,150	3,680	3,830	4,000	4,400
* Quarrying	680	698	726	790	870
- Manufacturing Industries	87,550	95,750	104,856	115,150	123,680
- Electricity, Gas and Water	6,300	6,470	6,462	7,068	7,160
- Construction	83,950	92,830	173,150	201,111	210,800
- Wholesale Retail Trade and Repairing Services	127,530	143,465	174,025	197,300	210,758
- Restaurants and Hotels	32,350	41,900	49,648	51,225	58,710
- Transports, Storage and Communication	41,275	56,329	57,860	68,057	69,869
- Real Estate and Business Services	15,465	20,536	22,726	24,267	28,380
- Social and Personal Services	29,950	33,462	34,282	39,200	41,910
The Financial Corporations Sector	**12,442**	**13,361**	**13,889**	**14,525**	**14,865**
Government Services Sector	**49,710**	**52,900**	**63,189**	**68,400**	**72,324**
- Domestic Services of Households	52,198	56,113	57,690	57,850	58,010
TOTAL	**550,190**	**627,051**	**771,978**	**859,481**	**912,723**

* Preliminary data
Source: Ministry of Planning

Issued Work Permits, Cards and Cancelled Sponsorships, Cards - Emirate of Dubai (2000-2004)					
TITLE	**2000**	**2001**	**2002**	**2003**	**2004**
Work permits					
Issued	67,400	77,149	151,252	239,189	297,730
Cancelled Sponsorships	56,898	52,353	71,858	90,950	111,664
Work Cards					
Issued	78,139	67,025	115,318	195,672	194,272
Cancelled	56,898	52,353	71,858	90,950	111,664

Source: Ministry of Labour and social Affairs

Foreign Trade by Sea Ports - Emirate of Dubai
(2004) - (Value in Million AED & Q. in Tonnes)

Title	Imports		Exports		Re-exports	
	Quantity	Value	Quantity	Value	Quantity	Value
Port Rashid	3,931,554	22,875	978,287	1,734	1,141,597	8,356
Jebel Ali Port	15,143,566	68,875	2,149,439	5,505	1,734,758	11,602
Hamriya Port	396,080	402	45,902	65	393,828	2,421
Dubai Creek	83,837	155	155,539	307	813,944	6,781
Total	19,555,037	92,307	3,329,167	7,611	4,084,127	29,160

Source: Ports, Customs & Free Zone Corporation

Quantity of Goods Discharged at Rashid and Jebel Ali Ports
(2000-2004) - (Unit: D / WT)

Title	2000	2001	2002	2003	2004
Quantity Discharged A-Containers					
- Imports	7,065,599	7,729,549	8,909,088	10,679,179	13,060,478
- Trans. Sh.	6,438,323	7,658,332	9,205,225	11,780,350	14,151,364
S. Total	13,503,922	15,387,881	18,114,313	22,459,529	27,211,842
B- General					
- General Cargo	2,450,486	2,765,993	3,441,897	4,224,304	5,238,910
- Bulk Cargo	3,764,312	3,403,407	4,111,838	4,098,637	5,214,928
S. Total	6,214,798	6,169,400	7,553,735	8,322,941	10,453,838
C- Petroleum					
- Oil	8,010,825	7,255,063	6,694,711	7,928,735	10,285,606
- Gases	242,261	316,262	331,490	328,361	355,496
- Asphalt	116,197	100,285	106,449	127,085	91,846
S. Total	8,369,283	7,671,610	7,132,650	8,384,181	10,732,948
G.Total (discharged)	28,088,003	29,228,891	32,800,698	39,166,651	48,398,628

Source: Ports, Customs & Free Zone Corporation

Quantity of Goods Loaded at Rashid and Jebel Ali Ports (2000-2004) - (Unit: D / WT)					
Title	2000	2001	2002	2003	2004
Quantity Loaded A-Containers					
- Exports	4,408,260	4,507,217	5,363,634	6,945,401	7,878,698
- Trans. Sh.	6,438,323	7,658,332	9,205,225	11,780,350	14,151,364
S. Total	**10,846,583**	**12,165,549**	**14,568,859**	**18,725,751**	**22,030,062**
B- General Goods					
- General Cargo	542,069	615,619	748,164	1,000,298	1,020,324
- Bulk Cargo	455,383	588,208	659,129	507,107	676,965
S. Total	**997,452**	**1,203,827**	**1,407,293**	**1,507,405**	**1,697,289**
C- Petroleum Oil					
- Oil	4,285,943	3,975,009	2,985,110	4,145,947	5,169,813
- Gases	109,979	136,605	69,736	80,588	63,751
S. Total	**4,395,922**	**4,111,614**	**3,054,846**	**4,226,535**	**5,233,564**
G. Total loaded	**16,239,957**	**17,480,990**	**19,030,998**	**24,459,691**	**28,960,915**
G. T. Dis. & Loaded	**44,327,960**	**46,709,881**	**51,831,696**	**63,626,343**	**77,359,543**

Source: Ports, Customs & Free Zone Corporation

Containers Discharged & Loaded at Rashid and Jebel Ali Ports (2000-2004) - (Unit: 20 foot equivalent units)

Title	2000	2001	2002	2003	2004
Discharged Containers					
Imports	634,136	694,656	817,245	986,850	1,228,630
Trans. Sh.	643,188	741,422	901,863	1,142,730	1,387,065
Empty Units	246,959	307,019	378,894	453,574	596,877
S. Total	**1,524,283**	**1,743,097**	**2,098,002**	**2,583,154**	**3,212,572**
Loaded Containers					
Exports	350,626	370,186	439,400	554,427	670,105
Trans. Sh.	644,919	747,302	902,457	1,136,290	1,384,668
Empty Units	539,040	641,234	754,406	878,083	1,161,536
S. Total	**1,534,585**	**1,758,722**	**2,096,263**	**2,568,800**	**3,216,309**
G. Total	**3,058,868**	**3,501,819**	**4,194,265**	**5,151,954**	**6,428,881**

Source: Ports, Customs & Free Zone Corporation

Vessels Calling to Rashid and Jebel Ali Ports by Type (2000-2004) (Unit.No.)

Type	2000	2001	2002	2003	2004
Containers Vessels	4,869	4,877	4,947	5,124	5,229
General Cargo Vessels	804	835	849	1,262	1,549
General Cargo/Container Vessels	45	65	55	92	96
Bulk Carriers	210	200	212	251	269
Car Carriers	361	456	580	602	700
Tankers	817	744	719	760	923
Livestock Carriers	22	24	27	24	20
Naval Visits, Vessels	282	183	335	308	312
Passengers Ships	265	435	419	380	413
Country Crafts	672	709	717	928	1,079
Others	2,597	2,765	2,917	3,501	3,445
Total	**10,944**	**11,293**	**11,777**	**13,232**	**14,035**

Sources: Ports, Customs & Free Zone Corporation

Title	Arrivals		Departures		Transit		Total	
Passengers Movement at Dubai International Airport by Type (2000-2004)- 2000 = 100								
2000	5,600,146	100	5,516,621	100	1,203,893	100	**12,320,660**	**100**
2001	6,212,379	111	6,188,432	112	1,107,212	92	**13,508,023**	**110**
2002	7,522,283	134	7,376,965	134	1,074,143	89	**15,973,391**	**130**
2003	8,651,712	154	8,523,354	155	887,278	74	**18,062,344**	**147**
2004	10,572,393	189	10,296,963	187	842,527	70	**21,711,883**	**176**

Source: Department of Dubai Civil Aviation

Title	Quantity of Discharged Goods		Quantity of Loaded Goods		Total	
Cargo Movement at Dubai International Airport (2000-2004) - (Quantity in Tonnes) - 2000=100						
2000	309,644	100	252,947	100	**562,591**	**100**
2001	349,653	113	261,214	103	**610,867**	**109**
2002	425,405	137	338,788	134	**764,193**	**136**
2003	505,336	163	423,422	167	**928,758**	**165**
2004	602,948	195	508,699	201	**1,111,647**	**198**

Source: Department of Dubai Civil Aviation

Dubai Shopping Festival Main Indicators - Emirate of Dubai (2000-2004)					
Title	**2000**	**2001**	**2002**	**2003**	**2004**
Festival Days	31	31	31	31	32
Total Visitors (Th.)	2,500	2,550	2,680	2,920	3,100
Daily Average of Visitors	80,600	82,300	86,500	94,194	96,875
Total Spending (Mn. AED)	4,310	4,500	4,600	5,120	5,800
Daily Average of Spending (Mn. AED)	139	145	148	165	181

Source: Department of Economic Development

References

A

- Abraaj Capital website
- ACNielsen consumer confidence report
- Airports Council International, report
- Al-Bayan *newspaper*
- Al Futtaim Group website
- Al-Hayat *newspaper*
- Al-Ittihad *newspaper*
- Al-Khaleej *newspaper*
- All-World-News website
- AM Best Company report
- AME Info website
- American Express Travel *magazine*
- Amlak Finance
- Anti-Monetary Laundering & Suspicious Cases Unit (AMLSC), report
- ARAB AD *magazine*
- Arab Bank for Investment and Foreign Trade, report
- Arab Business Intelligence Report (ABIR), published by Moutamarat and Pricewaterhouse Coopers
- Arab Competitiveness Report 2005, World Economic Froum Round Table
- Arab Health *magazine*
- Arab Media Forum
- Arab Medicare website
- Arab Monetary Fund, reports
- Arabian Business *magazine*
- Arabian Travel Market, Exhibition, 2006, handouts
- Asharq Al-Awsat *newspaper*
- Azal Group website

B

- Bahrain Tribune *newspaper*
- Banker *magazine*, The
- Banker Middle East *magazine*, The
- Banking and Finance, special report, published by Gulf News *newspaper*
- Bawadi Project Brochure

References

• British Embassy, statistical report
• Burj Al Arab, website
• Burj Dubai development, Fact Sheet
• Business Traveller *magazine*
• BusinessWeek *magazine*

C

• CABSAT 2006 Broadcasting Conference 2006, handouts
• Campaign Middle East *magazine*
• Canadian Embassy in Abu Dhabi, report
• Canadian Fraser Institute, report
• Capital Intelligence Agency, report
• Capital Markets Forum 2006 (GCC), handouts
• Central Bank of the UAE, reports and bulletins
• Chartered Insurance Institute (CII), report
• Christian Science Monitor *magazine* , The
• Cityscape Exhibition 2005, handouts
• Commercial Bank of Dubai website
• Construction Week *magazine*
• Country Brand Index 2005
• CSR: 2nd Middle East Summit 2005, handouts
• Culross Global Management (CGM) website

D

• Daily Star *newspaper*, The
• Daily Telegraph *newspaper*, The
• Definitive Meeting and Event Planners' Guide (Dubai 2006), The
• Deira City Center website
• Department of Civil Aviation (DCA)
• Department of Economic Development (DED), reports
• Department of Tourism and Commerce Marketing (DTCM), reports
• Destination Dubai, Tourism Manual 2006, published by Dubai Department of Tourism and Commerce Marketing (DTCM)
• DNATA website & brochures
• Dubai Aid City website

References

• Dubai Airport Free Zone Authority (DAFZA) website and brochure
• Dubai Aluminium (DUBAL) website
• Dubai Bank website
• Dubai Biotechnology and Research Park (Dubiotech) website
• Dubai Business Handbook 2006, published by DTCM
• Dubai Cargo Village website
• Dubai Chamber of Commerce and Industry (DCCI)
• Dubai City Guide website
• Dubai Diamond Exchange (DDE) website
• Dubai Duty Free (DDF)
• Dubai Energy website
• Dubai Festival City (DFC)
• Dubai Financial Market (DFM) reports & bulletins
• Dubai Financial Services Authority (DFSA)
• Dubai Flower Center brochure
• Dubai Gold and Commodities Exchange (DGCX)
• Dubai Headed For the Future, Special Report, published by Khaleej Times
• Dubai Healthcare City (DHCC) website
• Dubai Holding
• Dubai Humanitarian City (DHC) website
• Dubai Industrial City (DIC) website
• Dubai International Airport (DIA)
• Dubai International Airport, Yearbook & Directory 2006-2007
• Dubai International Capital (DIC) website
• Dubai International Convention & Exhibition Center (DICEC)
• Dubai International Financial Center (DIFC)
• Dubai International Financial Exchange (DIFX)
• Dubai Internet City website
• Dubai Investments website & brochures
• Dubai Investments Parks (DIP) website & brochures
• Dubai Islamic Bank
• Dubai Knowledge Village website
• Dubailand Announced Projects, Information and contact List
• Dubailand brochure
• Dubai Logistics City website

References

• Dubai Mall Brochure, The
• Dubai Marina website
• Dubai Maritime City website
• Dubai Media City (DMC) website
• Dubai Mercantile Exchange (DME) website
• Dubai Municipality website
• Dubai Multi Commodities Center (DMCC) website
• Dubai Municipality, Statistics Center – Statistical yearbook 2004, Emirate of Dubai
• Dubai Municipality, Statistics Center – Dubai In Figures 2005
• Dubai Naturalization and Residency Department, report
• Dubai Outsource Zone (DOZ) website
• Dubai Police website
• Dubai Ports World (DP World)
• Dubai Properties
• Dubai Shopping Festival (DSF) website
• Dubai Shopping Malls Group (DSMG), report
• Dubai Silicon Oasis website & brochure
• Dubai Sports City, brochure
• Dubai Summer Surprises (DSS) website
• Dubai Tea Trading Center (DTTC)
• Dubai Technology & Media Free Zone (TeCom) website & brochure
• Dubai Technology Park website
• Dubai World Trade Center (DWTC)
• Dyna Liners listing

E
• e-Government Official Portal (dubai.ae) website
• Economist Intelligence Unit (EIU) Report
• Economist magazine, The
• EFG-Hermes, reports and studies
• Emaar Properties
• Emarat Alyoum *newspaper*
• Emirates Airline
• Emirates Airline, Special Supplement (20th anniversary, 2005), published by Al-Khaleej
  newspaper

References

• Emirates Bank Group website
• Emirates Banks Association, annual report 2005
• Emirates Industrial Bank, report
• Emirates Institute for Financial and Banking Studies, publications, The
• Emirates Insurance Association, annual report 2005
• Emirates Network website, The
• Emirates Today *newspaper*
• Energy Information Administration (EIA), reports
• Entrepreneur ME *magazine*
• Entrepreneurs in Dubai, Supplement, published by Gulf Business Review
• Eqarat website
• Etisalat website
• Euromoney Country Risk Poll 2006
• Euromoney *magazine*
• Eurostat Trade Statistics

F

• Family Business Forum 2006, handouts
• FDI *magazine*
• Federal Association of the German Tourism Industry (BTW), report
• Figaro *newspaper*, Le
• Financial Stability Institute and Bank for International Settlements, survey
• Financial Times *newspaper*
• Fitch Ratings
• Forbes *magazine*
• Fox News website
• Franchise.com website
• Franchising Middle East Exhibition 2006, handouts

G

• GCC Economic Forum 2005, handouts
• Generation Group, DataBank
• Getyourmoneyworking website
• GITEX Exhibition 2005, handouts
• Global Competitiveness Report 2005-2006, World Economic Forum

References

- Global Information Technology Report 2005-2006, World Economic Forum
- Global Lodging Review, Deloitte and Smith Travel Research
- Global Logistics & Supply Chain Strategies (GLSCS) website
- Global Village website
- GODO Research Marketing Consultancy (GRMC), report
- GoDubai website
- Gold Field Mineral Services (GFMS), reports & surveys
- Growth Competitiveness Index 2005, World Economic Forum
- Guardian *newspaper*, The
- Guinness World Records 2006, The
- Gulf Business *magazine*
- Gulf Industry Food website
- Gulf Marketing Review *magazine*
- Gulf News *newspaper*
- Gulf Print Exhibition 2005, handouts
- Gulf Today *newspaper*

H

- Hong Kong Herald *newspaper*
- Hospitality Net website
- Hotelier Middle East *magazine*
- HSBC, reports
- HVS International, "The Dubai hotel market - Hot or soon to overheat?", 2005, report

I

- IFA Hotels & Resorts website
- IKEA Dubai website
- Independent *newspaper*, The
- Institute for International Research (IIR)
- International Advertising Association World Congress - IAA Conference (March 2006)
- International Council of Shopping Centers (ICSC) website
- International Finance Corporation (IFC)
- International Herald Tribune *newspaper*
- International Islamic Finance Forum 2006, handouts
- International Monetary Fund (IMF) report 2005

References

• Invest Dubai *magazine*
• Ipsos-Stat Researches & Surveys
• Islamic Finance Forum 2005, handouts
• Islamic Republic News Agency (IRNA) website
• Islamic Retail Banking Conference II 2005, handouts
• IT Risk Management Conference 2005, handouts

J
• Jadaf Dubai website
• Jebel Ali Free Zone Authority (JAFZA)
• Jumeirah Group website

K
• KAS Bank website
• Khaleej Times *newspaper*
• Korea Times *newspaper*, The

L
• Law Update newsletters, published by Al Tamimi and Company
• Leaders in Dubai Conference

M
• Mall of the Emirates website
• Mashreqbank website
• McKinsey Competitiveness Report 2005-2006, published by the WIBC
• Media and Marketing Show 2005, handouts
• Meed *magazine*
• Meeting Incentives Conferences Exhibitions (MICE) *magazine*, 2006
• Menareport website
• Middle East Council of Shopping Centers website
• Middle East Duty Free Association (MEDFA), report
• Middle East Insurance and Reinsurance Forum 2005, handouts
• Middle East Logistics website
• Middle East *magazine*
• Middle East North Africa Financial Network (Menafn) website

References

- Middle East Quality Association, report
- Ministry of Economy and Planning, reports
- Moody's Rating Reports
- Moto-With-Me report
- My Vision Book (by HH Sheikh Mohammed Bin Rashid Al Maktoum, Vice President & Prime Minister of the UAE and Ruler of Dubai)

N
- Nakheel
- National Bank of Abu Dhabi (NBAD), monthly bulletin
- National Bank of Dubai, reports
- National Bonds Corporation, website
- Networked Rediness Index, The, World Economic Forum
- New Republic *magazine*, The
- New York Times *newspaper*, The
- Newsweek *magazine*
- Nouvel Observateur *magazine*, Le

O
- Oman Insurance Company, website

P
- Peninsula *magazine*
- Ports, Customs & Free Zone Corporation
- PricewaterhouseCoopers, report
- Property Weekly *magazine*
- Property World Middle East *magazine*

R
- Reporters Without Borders (sans Frontières), 3rd annual worldwide index of press freedom
- Retail International (RI), report
- Retail ME *magazine*
- Retail Real Estate Forum & Exhibition 2005, handouts
- Reuters website
- Roads and Transport Authority

References

• Rotana Hotels website
• Rutgers University (State University of New Jersey), rating report

S
• Salama Islamic Arab Insurance Company
• Saneou El-Hadath *magazine*
• Seattle Times *newspaper*
• Shuaa Capital, monthly bulletins
• Standard & Poor's, report
• Standard Chartered Bank, reports
• Statisticsdubai website
• Strategiy.com website
• Sunday Herald *newspaper*

T
• Takaful-Re
• Tameer
• Tamweel website
• Tatweer website
• Telegraph *newspaper*
• Time *magazine*
• Times *newspaper*, The
• TradeArabia website
• Trends *magazine*
• TRI Hospitality Consulting, report

U
• UAE Banking Review
• UAE Banking, Special Report, Meed *magazine*
• UAE Business Forecast Report
• UAE Country Profile (March 2006), Library of Congress, Federal Research Division
• UAE Country Report, released by Oxford Business School
• UAE Economic & Strategic Outlook II, MacroEconomic Profile, published by Global Investment House
• UAE Free Zone Investment Guide

References

• UAE Industry Statistics Yearbook (2005), published by the Ministry of Finance & Industry
• UAE Interact website
• UAE Statistical Report, released by the Italian Commercial Centre (ICC)
• UAE Website Directory 2005-2006
• United Arab Emirates Yearbook 2006
• United Nations Conference on Trade and Development (UNCTAD), report
• United Nations Economic and Social Commission for Western Asia (ESCWA), report
• United Nations Human Development Index (HDI)
• United Nations Statistics Division, report
• USroom website

V

• Vanity Fair *magazine*
• Virgin Megastore

W

• Wall Street Journal, *newspaper*,The
• Washington Post *newspaper*, The
• Wikipedia website
• World Bank reports, The
• World Gold Council (WGC), report
• World Intellectual Property Organization, report
• World Islamic Banking Conference 2005, handouts
• World Takaful Conference 2006, handouts
• World Trade Organization (WTO), reports
• World Trade Point Federation, rating report
• World Travel and Tourism Council (WTTC), publications
• World Wealth report, published by Merrill Lynch and Capgemini

Y

• Young Arab Leaders, website

Z

• Zawya website

References

Websites

102749316

Government |

Department of Economic Development	www.dubaided.gov.ae
Dubai Chamber of Commerce & Industry	www.dcci.ae
Dubai City Guide	www.dubaicityguide.com
Dubai Civil Defense	www.dcd.gov.ae
Dubai Courts	www.djd.gov.ae
Dubai Customs	www.dxbcustoms.gov.ae
Dubai Development Board	www.dubaidb.gov.ae
Dubai Dry Docks	www.drydocks.gov.ae
Dubai E-Government	www.dubai.ae
Dubai Electricity & Water Authority	www.dewa.gov.ae
Dubai Government Excellence Program	www.dubaiexcellence.com
Dubai Land Department	www.dubailand.gov.ae
Dubai Municipality	www.dm.gov.ae
Dubai Naturalization & Residency Dept.	www.dnrd.gov.ae
Dubai Police	www.dubaipolice.gov.ae
Dubai Ports Authority	www.dpa.co.ae
Department of Health & Medical Services	www.dohms.gov.ae
Dept. of Tourism & Commerce Marketing	www.dubaitourism.co.ae
Dubai Real Estate Department	www.realestate-dubai.gov.ae
Dubai Transport	www.dubaitransport.gov.ae
Dubai World Trade Center	www.dwtc.com
Emirates General Petroleum Corporation	www.emarat.ae
Emirates Organization	www.emirates.org
Emirates Post	www.emiratespost.com
Federal Environmental Agency	www.fed.gov.ae
General Information Authority	www.gia.gov.ae
Etisalat	www.etisalat.co.ae
UAE Government	www.uae.gov.ae
UAE Interact	www.uaeinteract.com

Websites

Travel & Tourism |

Travel
Department of Civil Aviation	http://dca.dubai.ae
DNATA	www.dnata.com
Dubai Duty Free	www.dubaidutyfree.com
Dubai International Airport	www.dubaiairport.com
Emirates Airline	www.emirates.com

Entertainment
Dubai Shopping Festival	www.mydsf.com
Dubai Summer Surprises	www.mydsf.com
Nad Al Sheba Club	www.dubaigolf.com/nasc
Ski Dubai	www.skidxb.com
Wild Wadi	www.wildwadi.com
Wonderland	www.wonderlanduae.com

Sports & Events
Dubai Country Club	www.dubaicountryclub.com
Dubai Desert Classic	www.dubaidesertclassic.com
Dubai Golf	www.dubaigolf.com
Dubai International Marine Club	www.dimc-uae.com
Dubai Rugby 7's	www.dubairugby7s.com
Dubai Tennis Championships	www.dubaitennischampionships.com
Dubai Tennis Open	www.dubaitennisopen.com
Dubai World Cup	www.dubaiworldcup.com
Emirates Karting Club	www.emirateskartingclub.com

Hotels
Al Bustan Rotana	www.albustanrotanahoteldubai.com
Al Maha Desert Resort	www.al-maha.com
Al Murooj Rotana	www.almuroojrotanahoteldubai.com
Al Qasr	www.madinatjumeirah.com/al_qasr
Bab Al Shams	www.jumeirahbabalshams.com
Burj Al Arab	www.burj-al-arab.com
Crowne Plaza	www.crowneplaza.com

Websites

Dubai Marine Beach Resort & Spa	www.dxbmarine.com/dbrindex.html
Dusit Hotels	www.dusit.com
Emirates Towers	www.jumeirahemiratestowers.com
Fairmont	www.fairmont.com/dubai
Grand Hyatt	www.hyatt.com
Grosvenor House Dubai	www.grosvenorhouse-dubai.com
Habtoor Grand Resort	http://grandjumeirah.habtoorhotels.com
Hilton Dubai	www.hilton.com
Hyatt Regency Dubai	http://dubai.regency.hyatt.com
InterContinental	www.intercontinental.com
Jumeirah Beach	www.jumeirahbeachhotel.com
JW Marriott	http://marriott.com
Kempinski	www.kempinski.com
Madinat Jumeirah	www.madinatjumeirah.com
Mina A'Salam	www.madinatjumeirah.com/mina_a_salam
Mövenpick	www.moevenpick-hotels.com
Novotel World Trade Center	www.novotel.com
One & Only Royal Mirage Dubai	www.oneandonlyresorts.com
Ritz-Carlton Dubai	www.ritzcarlton.com
Rotana Hotels	www.rotana.com
Royal Meridien, Le	www.leroyalmeridien-dubai.com
Royal Mirage	www.royalmiragedubai.com
Shangri-La	www.shangri-la.com
Sofitel	www.sofitel.com
Shopping	
Al Ghurair City	www.alghuraircity.com
Burjuman Center	www.burjuman.com
Deira City Center	www.deiracitycentre.com
Ibn Battutta Mall	www.ibnbattutamall.com
Lamcy Plaza	www.lamcyplaza.com
Mall of the Emirates	www.malloftheemirates.com
Mazaya Center	www.mazayacentre.com
Mercato Mall	www.mercatoshoppingmall.com
Reef Mall	www.reefmall.com

Websites

Souq Madinat Jumeirah   www.madinatjumeirah.com/shopping
Town Center   www.towncentrejumeirah.com
Wafi Shopping Center   www.wafi.com

Ongoing Projects |

Burj Dubai   www.burjdubai.com
Business Bay   www.businessbay.ae
Dubai Festival City   www.dubaifestivalcity.com
Dubai International City   www.internationalcity.ae
Dubai Investments Park   www.dipark.com
Dubai Lagoon   www.dubailagoon.com
Dubai Mall   www.thedubaimall.com
Dubai Marina   www.dubai-marina.com
Dubai Metro   http://vgn.dm.gov.ae/DMEGOV/dm-mp-metro
Dubai Pearl   www.dubaipearl.com
Dubai Waterfront   www.dubaiwaterfront.ae
Dubai World Central   www.dubaiworldcentral.com
Dubai World Trade Center Residence   www.theresidence-dwtc.ae
Dubailand   www.dubailand.ae
Jumeirah Beach Residence   www.jbr.ae
Jumeirah Lake Towers   www.jumeirahlaketowers.com
Lagoons, The   www.lagoons.ae
Old Town   www.theoldtown.ae
Palm Jumeirah, The   www.thepalm.ae
Palm Jebel Ali, The   www.nakheel.ae
Plam Deira, The   www.nakheel.ae
Rêve, Le   www.lerevedubai.com
Rose Rotana Suites   www.rosetower.net
World, The   www.theworld.ae

Websites

Free Zones |

Dubai Airport Free Zone Authority	www.dafza.gov.ae
Dubai Biotechnology & Research Park	www.dubiotech.com
Dubai Cargo Village	www.dubaicargovillage.com
Dubai Cars & Automotive Zone	www.ducamz.co.ae
Dubai Flower Center	www.dubaiflowercentre.com
Dubai Internet City	www.dubaiinternetcity.com
Dubai Healthcare City	www.dhcc.ae
Dubai Humanitarian city	www.dhc.ae
Dubai Industrial City	www.dubaiindustrialcity.ae
Dubai Knowledge Village	www.kv.ae
Dubai Logistics City	www.dubailogisticscity.com
Dubai Maritime City	www.dubaimaritimecity.ae
Dubai Media City	www.dubaimediacity.com
Dubai Outsource zone	www.doz.ae
Dubai Silicon Oasis	www.dso.ae
Dubai Studio City	www.dubaistudiocity.com
Dubai Technology Park	www.tp.ae
Gold & Diamond Park	www.goldanddiamondpark.com
International Media Production Zone	www.impz.ae
Jebel Ali Free Zone	www.jafza.co.ae

Banking & Finance |

Abraaj Capital	www.abraaj.com
Amlak Finance	www.amlakfinance.com
Commercial Bank of Dubai	www.cbd.co.ae
Commercial Bank International	www.cbiuae.com
Dubai Bank	www.dubaibank.ae
Dubai Diamond Exchange	www.dde.ae
Dubai Financial Market	www.dfm.co.ae
Dubai Financial Services Authority	www.dfsa.ae
Dubai Gold & Commodities Exchange	www.dgcx.ae

Websites

Dubai International Financial Center	www.difc.ae
Dubai International Financial Exchange	www.difx.ae
Dubai Islamic Bank	www.alislami.co.ae
Dubai Islamic Insurance & Reinsurance – AMAN	www.aman.ae
Dubai Mercantile Exchange	www.dubaimerc.com
Dubai Multi Commodities Center	www.dmcc.ae
Dubai National Insurance & Reinsurance	www.dnirc.com
Emirates Banks Association	www.eba-ae.com
Emirates Bank Group	www.emiratesbank.ae
Emirates Insurance Company	www.emirates-ins.com
Islamic Arab Insurance Company – Salama	www.salama.ae
Mashreqbank	www.mashreqbank.com
National Bank of Dubai	www.nbd.com
National Bonds Corporation	www.nationalbonds.ae
Oman Insurance Company	www.oicem.com
Shuaa Capital	www.shuaacapital.com
Takaful Re	www.takaful-re.ae
Tamweel	www.tamweel.ae
UAE Central Bank	www.uaecb.gov.ae

Business & Companies |

Ahmed Seddiqi & Sons	www.seddiqi.com
Al Futtaim Group	www.futtaim.com
Al Ghandi Group	www.alghandi.com
Al Ghurair Group	www.alghurair.com
Al Habtoor Group	www.habtoor.com
Al Nabooda Group	www.alnabooda.com
Al Sayegh Brothers	www.alsayeghbrothers.com
Al Shirawi Group	www.alshirawi.com
Al Tayer Group	www.altayer.com
Belhasa Group	www.belhasa.com
Dubai Holding	www.dubaiholding.com
Dubai Aluminium (Dubal)	www.dubal.ae

Websites

Dubai Investments	www.dubaiinvestments.com
Emaar	www.emaar.com
Gargash Enterprises	www.gargash.mercedes-benz.com
I & M Galadari Group	www.imgaladari.com
Juma Al Majid Group	www.al-majid.com
Majid Al Futtaim Group	www.majidalfuttaim.com
Nakheel	www.nakheel.ae
Union Properties	www.up.ae

Education |

American School of Dubai	www.asdubai.org
American University in Dubai	www.aud.edu
British University in Dubai, The	www.buid.ac.ae
Dubai College	www.dubaicollege.org
Dubai Modern High School	www.modernhighschool.com
Dubai University College	www.duc.ac.ae
Higher Colleges of Technology	www.hct.ac.ae
Jumeirah Primary School	www.jpsdubai.com
UAE University	www.uaeu.ac.ae

Embassies & Councils |

American Business Council	www.abcdubai.com
Australian Embassy	www.uae.embassy.gov.au
British Business Group	www.britbiz-uae.com
British Embassy	www.britain-uae.org
Canadian Embassy	www.international.gc.ca/abudhabi
Finland Embassy	www.finland.ae
French Embassy	www.ambafrance-eau.org
German Business Council	www.gbc-dubai.com

Websites

German Embassy	www.abu-dhabi.diplo.de
Indian Consulate-General	www.cgidubai.com
Indian Embassy	www.indembassyuae.org
Indonesian Embassy	www.indonesianembassy.ae
Iranian Embassy	www.iranembassy.org.ae
Iranian Business Council	www.ibcuae.org
Pakistan Consulate-General	www.pakcgdubai.org.ae/assn.htm
Royal Norwegian Embassy	www.norway.ae/info/embassy.htm
Singapore Consulate-General	www.mfa.gov.sg/dubai
South African Embassy	www.southafrica.ae
Swedish Business Council	www.swedchamb.com
US Embassy	uae.usembassy.gov
Yemen Embassy	www.yemen-embassy.org.ae

Media |

7Days	www.7days.ae
Al-Bayan Newspaper	www.albayan.ae
Al Ittihad Newspaper	www.alittihad.ae
Al Khaleej	www.alkhaleej.ae
Dubai Press Club	www.dpc.org.ae
Dubai TV	www.dubaitv.gov.ae
Emirates Today	www.emiratestodayonline.com
Emarat Alyoum	www.emaratalyoum.com
Gulf News	www.gulfnews.com
Gulf Business Review	www.gulfbusiness.com
Gulf Marketing Review	www.gmr-online.com
Khaleej Times	www.khaleejtimes.com
One TV	www.onetv.ae
Sama Dubai TV	www.samadubai.ae

Websites

5   3
4   3   5
3   5   4   1
4   3   5   5   4
3   2   1   1   6   4   6
4   8   9   7   0   1
4   5   5   4   0   5   4   5
0   5   5   4   6   5
3   5   4   7   6   0   4   4   6
5   7   9   8   0   2
1   6   1   1   6
5   6   5   0   1   2
6   8
6   5   1   5
3   7   1   0   1   7   8
3   5   4   0
5   4   0   3   5   4
0   6   4   4
0   7   5
0   6   5   7
2   1   2   0   1   3   5
1   3   5   4
0   3   5   7   5
0   3   5   4
1   5   6
7   8   1   3   1   0   5   4
4   1   5   6   4   0   3   4   5
0   3   5   4   7   8   0   3   3   5   3   5   0
0   3   4   3   5   2   8   7   3   2   2   3   1   0   3   4   6   3
1   6   5   5   4   4   5   4   6   5
0   3   4   1   0   5   6   1   6
0   6   5   4

Index

0216742384

Index

Index

Index

Index

Index

Index

Index

Index

Index

About
BEIRUT INFORMATION & STUDIES CENTER - BISC
and BUSINESS INFO - BI

⣿ BISC

Established in 1995, Beirut Information and Studies Center – BISC is a research center that offers studies, analytical reports, business intelligence, strategic communications, daily business monitoring, country & industry reviews, business lobbying and media industry expertise.

Financial & Business publishing is a major part of BISC's core business. This field includes Creative Writing, Content & Publishing Consultancy, coupled with the know-how in establishing Corporate Media Units, Newspapers, Periodicals and a variety of publications.

Our competitive advantage is the BISC Team. We have worked hard to attract and retain the best Economists, Researchers, Business Analysts, Communication Strategists, Journalists, Financial & Business Creative Writers and Translators that are highly recognized in their respective fields.

BISC has three Corporate Divisions: BISC Research, BISC Communications and BISC Publishing.

For more information, kindly visit our website www.bisc.com.lb

BUSINESS INFO
A member of BISC Group

"Business Info" - BI, a Dubai-based Research House, is specialized in Strategic Information Analysis, Publishing & Media Consultancy, providing clients with premium quality information-based products & services, selective and well-researched content.

Our specialities extend to "Publishing" Strategies, Feasibility Studies and Consultancy for books, guides and periodicals. Also, in co-operation with BISC Group's divisions, BI has the ability and skills to provide a wide range of services that BISC offers, with speciality in Arabic Business & Financial Copywriting.

In today's information age, the greatest business challenge is to collect, filter and analyze all of the multiplying daily information and construct an indispensible corporate asset.
"Business Info" is your solution for Information Anxiety.

For more information, kindly visit our website www.businessinfo.ae

This Book is available for purchase at BISC
& "Business Info" offices in Beirut and Dubai:

BISC

Beirut-Lebanon
Tel: +961 1 355 111
Fax: +961 1 355 110
bisc@bisc.com.lb

BUSINESS INFO
A member of BISC Group

Dubai-UAE
Tel: +971 4 3073723
      +971 50 2266412
Fax: +971 4 3215202
info@businessinfo.ae